Essential computing skills for working women or returners

Everything you need to know to use computers in the workplace

JACKIE SHERMAN

howtobooks

Published by How To Books Ltd,
3 Newtec Place, Magdalen Road,
Oxford OX4 1RE, United Kingdom.
Tel: (01865) 793806. Fax: (01865) 248780.
Email: info@howtobooks.co.uk
http://www.howtobooks.co.uk

First published 2005

British Library Cataloguing in Publication Data.
A catalogue record for this book is available from the British Library.

Produced for How To Books by Deer Park Productions, Tavistock
Typeset by Kestrel Data, Exeter, Devon
Cover design by Baseline Arts Ltd, Oxford
Printed and bound by Bell & Bain Ltd., Glasgow

NOTE: The material contained in this book is set out in good faith for general guidance
and no liability can be accepted for loss or expense incurred as a result of relying in particular
circumstances on statements made in the book. Laws and regulations are complex and liable
to change, and readers should check the current position with the relevant authorities before
making personal arrangements.

Contents

Introduction   **1**

    What do employers look for?   1

    What you need to know   2

    Using this book   2

1 Getting Started   **5**

    Logging in   5

    Computerised filing systems   6

    Creating folders on the desktop   7

    Using Windows Explorer   10

    Creating folders when saving   10

      Save As   12

2 Taking Control   **13**

    Special keys on the keyboard   13

    Toolbars and buttons   15

    Missing items   18

    Setting defaults   18

    Carry out a search   19

    Organising the view   22

      Files   22

      Page   23

    Opening files   24

    Using Help   25

      Question box   26

      Microsoft Help   26

      Tabs   26

      Office Assistant   27

      What's This?   27

3	**Word processing**	**28**
	A word about grammar (Business English)	28
	Starting new paragraphs	28
	Formal/informal English	29
	Semi-colons	29
	Colons	30
	Apostrophes	30
	Letters and memos	31
	Templates	31
	Logos and watermarks	34
	AutoText	37
	Automatic corrections	38
	Unwanted capital letters	40
	Dates	40
	International characters	40
	Mail merge	41
	Labels and envelopes	47
	Minutes of meetings	47
	Creating numbered lists	48
	Long documents	49
	Spelling	50
	Page numbers	50
	Headers and footers	51
	Move text (Cut and Paste)	52
	Selecting a large block of text	53
	Find or replace text	53
	Page and sections breaks	54
	Import files and objects	55
	Styles	57
	Table of contents	58
	Format Painter	60
	Index	60
	Sharing documents	61
	Tabs	62
	Amendments	63
	Tables	64
	Create a table	64
	Edit a table	65
	Table formats	67

Sorting		68
Calculations in tables		68
Changing text to tables		70
Publicity material		71
Text types		71
Dropped capitals		72
Pictures		72
Borders		76
Columns		77
Bullet formats		78
WordArt		78
Macros		80
Symbols and special characters		82
Detecting other people's settings		83
Key strokes		83
Menu options		83
4	**Spreadsheets and Charts**	**85**
	A few words about using numbers	86
	BODMAS	86
	Percentage	87
	Protecting cells	89
	Functions	90
	IF function	92
	Importing data	94
	Copying within Excel	94
	Inserting new columns or rows	95
	Absolute cells	96
	Naming cells	97
	Absolute cell reference	98
	Formats	99
	Error messages	99
	Customised dates	99
	Column headings	101
	Printing	102
	Give it a tick	103
	Create a series	104
	Working with worksheets	104
	Freeze panes	104

Naming sheets	106
Formulae across sheets and files	106
Arranging Windows	107
Finding information	107
Re-ordering entries	108
Updating entries	108
Using a form	109
Searching	110
Pivot tables	111
Design the table	111
Analyse the data	113
Calculations	114
Formatting	115
Charts	115
Change chart type	116
Add labels	117
Scale	118
Change data	118
Trendlines	122
Formatting lines and markers	122
Printing charts	123
5 Relational Databases	**124**
A brief overview	124
Primary key	125
Entering and amending records	125
Field properties	126
Replacing entries	128
Sorting records	129
Forms	130
Searching	130
Designing a query	132
Regular searches	135
Reports	136
Reports created automatically	136
Reports using the Wizard	137
Customising a report	140
Linking tables	142
Adding a primary key	142

Copying data   144
   Word processing   144
   Spreadsheets   145
   Mail merge   145
Importing data from elsewhere   145

6   The Internet and World Wide Web   **149**
Downloading   150
Internet v. Intranet   150
The browser window   150
Saving web pages   151
Saving pictures   152
Web addresses (URLs)   152
Basic information websites   153
Search engines   154
   Finding the information   156
   Directory search   156
Favorites   156
   Adding   157
   Visiting   158
   Organising   158
History   159
Video conferencing   159
   How it works   160
   Problems   160

7   E-mails and Diary Planning   **161**
   Start up   163
   Relationships   163
The Calendar   164
   Views   164
   Appointments   164
   Recurrent appointments   165
   Meeting invitations   166
   Printing   167
Tasks   168
Notes   169
Contacts   169
   Add an address   169

Group (distribution) mailing lists — 170
E-mails — 172
Addresses — 172
Creating messages — 172
Recall address from Contacts — 174
Blind copies for confidential messages — 174
Responding to messages — 174
Attaching files to e-mails — 175
Signatures — 178
Message options — 180
Out of Office messages — 180
Managing messages — 181
Archive old messages — 182
Message rules — 185
Searching — 190

8 Zipping (Compressing) files — **192**
Using Windows XP — 192
Compressing files — 192
Resizing pictures — 194
Reading zipped files — 194
Using WinZip — 196
Creating an archive — 196
Adding files — 197
Reading zipped files — 199

9 Digital Cameras — **200**
The basics — 200
Memory — 200
Resolution — 200
Taking pictures — 201
Image file types — 201
On the computer — 201
Viewing pictures — 202
Saving — 203
Toolbars and menus — 203
Cropping — 203
Rotating — 204
Adding text — 205

Automatic adjustments   206
Effects   207
Resizing   207
Printing   208

10 Scanners   **210**
Optical Character Recognition (OCR)   210
To scan a picture   213
Image editing   213
Add images to other documents   215

11 Creating Your Own CDs   **216**
How CDs are created   216
Types of CD   216
Using Windows XP   217
Alternative software   221

12 Presentations   **224**
Managing slides   225
Slide order   226
New slides   226
Making changes   227
Text   227
Text levels   229
Objects   229
Diagrams   230
Charts   231
Backgrounds   232
Colours and fills   232
Design templates   235
Drawings   235
Speaker's notes   236
Master slides   237
Printing   238
Slide shows   239
Timings   239
Effects   240

13 Desktop Publishing   **247**

The basics   247
Pages   248
Columns   248
Linking text boxes   249
Using ready-made designs   250
Adding or amending the contents   253
Printing   253

14 PDF files   **254**

Downloading PDF files   255
Moving through a document   256
Views   257
Copying contents of a PDF file   258

15 Relevant qualifications   **259**

New CLAIT   259
ECDL   260
Open College Network   260
LearnDirect   261

Index   263

Introduction

WHAT DO EMPLOYERS LOOK FOR?

Whether you want to return to work, change job or simply develop your career, you will be aware that a major revolution has taken place in the field of computing. Today, computers are an intrinsic part of most higher level professions and nearly all the jobs open to you if you are not offering specialised professional or technical qualifications still demand 'computer literacy' or 'good IT skills'. So what do these phrases mean in real terms?

They are simply another way of saying that the jobs require confidence in using a computer and, in most cases, a working knowledge of the *Microsoft Windows* operating system and Office products such as *Access*™ (databases), *Excel*™ (spreadsheets and charts), *Word*™ (word processing) or *PowerPoint*™ (presentations). As most companies use e-mail for communicating and many have their own Websites, they will also require you to have an understanding of the Internet and World Wide Web and perhaps know how to use *Outlook*™ (an e-mail and diary management system).

Along with this knowledge, you need to be familiar with the keyboard; it helps if you have reasonable (but not 'super-fast') typing speeds; and you must be able to write clear and accurate English.

Even if your organisation uses an alternative to Windows PCs e.g. the Apple Mac, or asks for related skills such as audio typing (creating documents dictated via an audio cassette), once you have mastered the most common computer packages, an employer will be happy to train you further as you should find learning extra skills or working with new software relatively straightforward.

WHAT YOU NEED TO KNOW

There are hundreds of books on computing and IT in the bookshops, but very few are aimed specifically at those in general or administrative positions or, particularly, women returning to work. Having trained hundreds of office workers and women returners, it became clear to me that a single book was needed covering every aspect of general computing that you are likely to face.

Not only do you need to know how to set out long documents, create a spreadsheet, search a database and attach files to e-mails, nowadays you are also likely to be asked to find information stored as a PDF file, save work onto a CD, edit pictures taken using the office camera, scan in images to incorporate into a newsletter, add sound effects to a presentation and even set up a video conference.

Hopefully, this book will give you the confidence and provide all the guidance you need to carry out the many and varied tasks you may be asked to perform.

USING THIS BOOK

If you are returning after a career break: whatever post you might have held before leaving work to bring up a family or look after a relative, and even if it involved some computing, you may be worried that your skills and knowledge are now out-of-date and that it will be hard to compete in the market place.

If you are in work: it can be daunting to be asked to carry out tasks for which you feel unprepared, and where there is no time for the necessary training that you need.

This book has been written to address both these concerns:

a) Work through it at home well before the application process gets underway so that you can feel confident you are truly computer literate and will be prepared for the range of IT demands you may face once you start your new job; and

b) Keep it next to your computer at work, to use as a reference guide if you suddenly need to carry out an unfamiliar or complex task on the computer that you haven't met before.

To update yourself thoroughly, the ideal would be to take a computing course at a local college or community education centre, but if you cannot do this because of work commitments, childcare or other considerations, it is perfectly possible to teach yourself computing at home. Many families now own a computer, but if you don't have access to one at all, there are drop-in centres in libraries, village halls or Internet cafes where it may be free or comparatively cheap for you to spend an hour or so each week brushing up your skills.

At the end of the book, you will find information on some of the more common IT qualifications accepted by employers today as evidence of computer literacy. However, it is *not* necessary to have any of these if you are applying for jobs which simply ask for good IT skills. As long as you include on your CV the names of all the software packages you can use e.g. *Microsoft Word*™ and *Excel*, and can describe some of the tasks you can now perform on a computer such as searching the Internet for information, word processing documents and sending and receiving e-mails, this should be quite adequate.

The book assumes that you have a very basic knowledge of computers i.e. you can use a mouse to select and open applications, understand how to use the keyboard and printer and have carried out simple word processing or similar activities. If you have never, ever used a computer before, it is a good idea to find a very basic introductory book aimed at complete beginners, to help you get started.

Although the material in this book is based on *Windows 2000*™ or *XP*™ operating systems and *Microsoft Office 2000*™ or *2002 (XP)*™ software, you should find it easy to transfer its contents to *Windows 98*™ or *ME*™ machines or earlier versions of *Office*, if these are the ones you have at home or that are used by your new employer.

Getting Started

LOGGING IN

In most organisations, your computer will be on a network and access will be restricted to a personal area or certain authorised parts of the system. To start work, you will have to follow the procedure known as logging in. This means typing in a username (your I.D.) and password in the appropriate boxes.

You may be provided with a username by your employer so that it follows company conventions e.g. your initial and the first 4 letters of your surname. (Paula MacKay would therefore have the username **pmack**). This can be typed in upper or lower case letters as it is 'case *in*sensitive.' As your username will be widely known or easy to guess, you will also need to choose a password that remains secret. It is the combination of username and password that allows you access to your area on the network.

When choosing passwords, there are several golden rules:

1. Passwords are 'case sensitive' so make sure you always type any capitals carefully: note that you won't actually see them on screen to check as you are only shown *****. Ideally, combine upper and lower case letters and numbers e.g. **sail4Home3**.

2. Don't tell anyone your password or use words that will be easy to guess – so *don't* choose the name of your house, partner or new puppy that everyone in the office will be familiar with.

3. Change your password regularly – there may be an option to do this in the logging in window. In some cases, the company provides you with your first password and then this must be changed by you straight away. (If you worry about forgetting new passwords, simply change one character each time e.g. a number or capital letter and write down *this* character only. Someone finding *G* or *7* on a piece of paper will not be able to do much with it.)

4. Remember to log off after every computer session or another member of staff may gain access to your work.

COMPUTERISED FILING SYSTEMS

Programs and files can be stored in a number of areas:

Non-removable storage:

◆ On the hard disk inside the computer you are physically working at, which is usually referred to as the C: drive.

◆ On a remote computer (known as a server) in another drive that may be labelled S, T or J etc. depending on how computers are organised within your company.

Removable storage:

◆ On optical CDs placed in the D: drive of your machine.

◆ On 3½ floppy disks placed in the A: drive – although these are now being phased out as they are prone to virus infection and can only store a limited number of files.

Wherever you are directed to store your work, a folder will usually have been set aside for this purpose labelled My Documents. As you create more and more files, it is sensible to organise them systematically. Make named folders inside My Documents to group related files together and help you locate them again quickly. This can be done either from the desktop or within the program you are using, at the same time that you save your work.

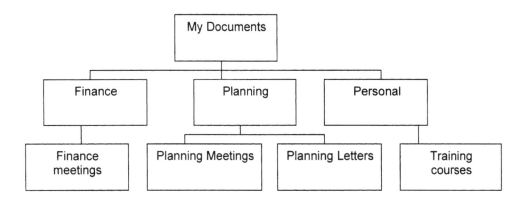

CREATING FOLDERS ON THE DESKTOP

1. To create a folder labelled *Planning* inside My Documents, open My Computer first from the desktop or **Start** menu or go straight to My Documents if there is an icon or link provided. You will see all the files you have created so far listed in the window.

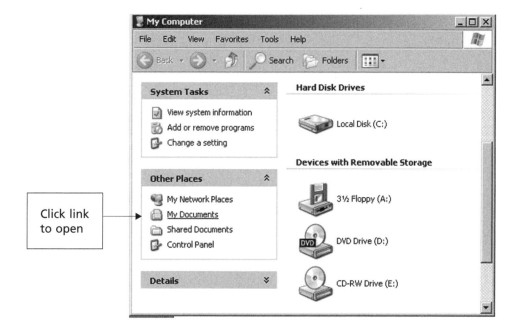

2. Click the *Make a New Folder* link in the left-hand pane (XP computers) or open the **File** menu and select **New – Folder.**

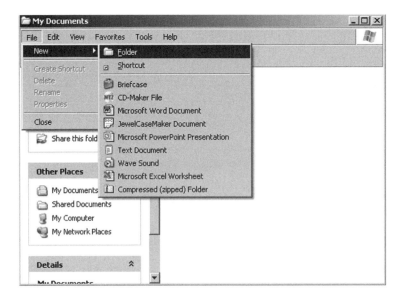

3. A yellow folder will appear in the window with the title New Folder showing against a blue background. Type *Planning* directly over the name and then press Enter to complete the naming process. (If you make a mistake, right-click the folder[1] and select *Rename*.)

4. To create further sub-folders such as *Planning Letters* or *Planning Meetings*, double-click to open the parent folder and then repeat the process.

[1]Clicking the right button on the mouse opens a short menu of options related to the position of the pointer on the screen.

5. To move planning-related files previously saved in My Documents into the *Planning* folder, find any in the window and either drag them directly into the folder or click them and then right-click if necessary to select the *Move this file* option.

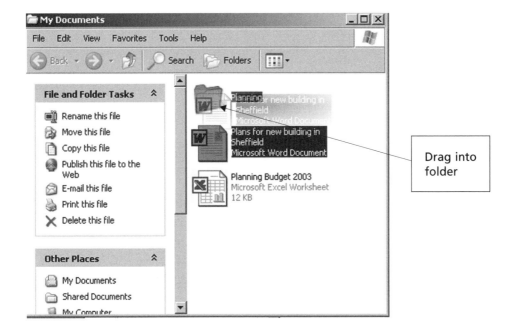

6. In the list of destination folders, click *Planning* and then the Move button and the file will be moved automatically. You may first need to click a + sign next to My Documents to reveal the folders inside. (The + sign will now change to a – sign.)

USING WINDOWS EXPLORER

7. A different way to move files into folders or sub-folders is to click the button labelled Folders. This opens the Explorer window that reveals all the drives, folders and sub-folders in your computer system. Once again, any folders containing sub-folders will show a + sign, so click this to expand the structure.

8. To move any files, you must be able to see the destination folder in the Folders list. Now click a folder in the left-hand Folders list to reveal its contents in the right-hand pane. Select the file you want to move and then drag it across the divide to the new destination folder showing on the left. Let go when the folder turns blue and the file will be dropped inside.

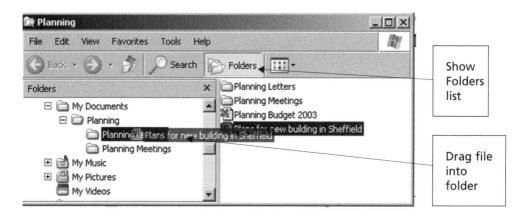

CREATING FOLDERS WHEN SAVING

1. When creating work, you will click the Save button 💾 to save a copy safely in a selected folder. The automatic (default) choice which will show in the Save in: box is likely to be My Documents, or the last folder you were working with. If you open in a sub-folder, click the Up arrow to move to higher level folders.

2. To save a document into a new *Planning Budgets* sub-folder that has not yet been created, drop down the list in the Save in: box to locate My Documents (or click the link in the Places Bar) and then double-click the *Planning* folder showing in the main window. It should now appear in the Save in: box.

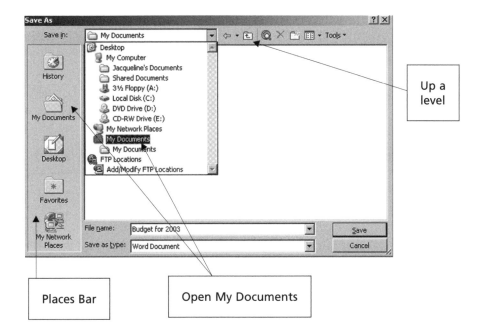

3. Click the *Create New Folder* button and type the name *Planning Budgets* in the box that appears.

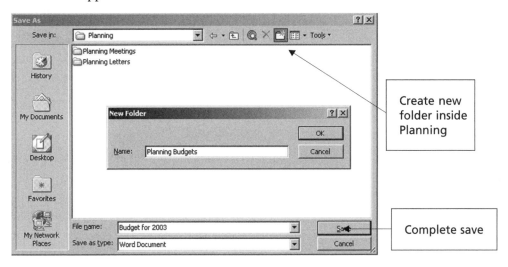

4. Click *OK* and check that the new sub-folder is now showing in the Save in: box. If not, double-click and it will open. When you click the *Save* button, your document will be saved directly into *Planning Budgets*.

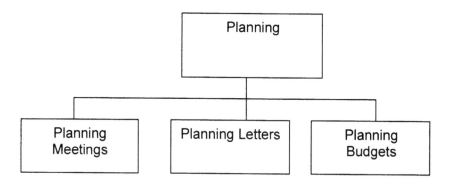

Save As

To save different versions of the same document, you need to distinguish between them. Either save them with a different name, or into a different folder.

Clicking the *Save* button will update your current document and overwrite the original, so open the Save As box by selecting this option from the **File** menu. Now you can amend the file name or change the location in the Save in: window before clicking *Save*.

$$\left(\begin{array}{c} 2 \end{array}\right)$$

Taking Control

Many computer users let the machine rule their lives and accept basic settings and standard screen layouts, even if these are difficult to work with. This chapter will put things right, giving you the confidence to re-assert your authority over the machine. You will then be able to carry out tasks more efficiently, correct errors, find missing items and receive help when you need it.

SPECIAL KEYS ON THE KEYBOARD

You may be familiar with the main keys on the keyboard, but have probably ignored many round the edge. However, these can be useful if you are in a hurry or want to find an alternative method for carrying out a task.

Number pad: if you prefer, you can use this block for entering numbers, mathematical operators such as * (multiply) or / (divide), and for pressing Enter. Make sure that a light shows the pad is on, or press Num Lock if you find no numbers appear as you type. Instead, you may find 7 takes you to the start of any line (the Home key), 1 takes you to the end of the line (the End key) and 9 and 3 take you up or down the page. These keys are also available in the block above the arrow (cursor) keys.

Overtyping: If you find letters are replaced when you try to insert new text, you have probably hit the Insert key by mistake and moved into overtyping. Return to normal by pressing the Insert key again.

Function keys: the top row of keys all begin with an F. Each one is a shortcut to a different task, depending on the package you are using, although F1 will always open the Help menu and F12 will open the Save As dialog box.[2]

Try pressing one or more of these keys when word processing or using *Excel* or *PowerPoint* to find out if they have a use e.g. in *Word*, F5 opens the *Find and Replace* dialog box and F7 starts the spell checker. In *Excel*, F2 will allow you to edit entries and in *PowerPoint*, F5 starts a slideshow.

Ctrl and Alt: Sometimes, a menu is not available and you will need to use the keyboard to carry out an action. Here are some shortcuts using Ctrl and another key. Select your entries, hold down Ctrl and press:

B – Bold
I – Italic
U – Underline
2 – Double space
1 – Single space
C – Copy
V – Paste
X – Cut

You can also carry out these general tasks:

N – Start a new document
P – Print dialog box
O – Open dialog box
S – Save your work (update if the file is already named, NOT Save As)
Z – Undo the last action

[2]Any window offering options that opens via a menu is known as a 'dialog box'.

Alt plus a key will replace the mouse if you want to open a menu. Each menu has one letter underlined, so Alt plus this letter will open the menu e.g. F for File, O for Format and A for Table.

Having opened the menu, key in the underlined letter to open the dialog box e.g. with the File menu open in *Word*, P opens the print box and with the Insert menu open, U opens the page numbers box.

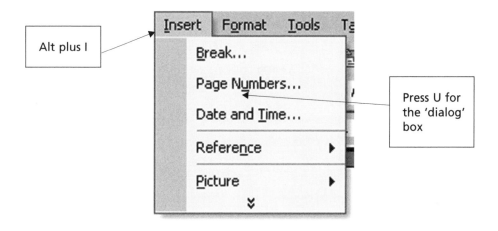

TOOLBARS AND BUTTONS

Don't waste time opening menus when carrying out common actions such as starting a new document, saving, printing or finding a saved file – it is much quicker to use the toolbar buttons. If you aren't sure which is which, rest your mouse pointer over the button to see a definition.

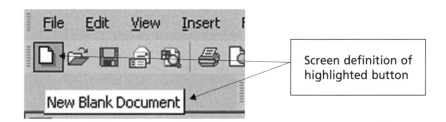

Just to confuse you, not all the buttons will be visible at one time as Microsoft uses 'intelligent' toolbars to limit the display and only shows recently used or basic buttons. You will also discover that sometimes a whole toolbar suddenly disappears.

Find a missing toolbar: right-click an empty space at the end of any toolbar and you will be offered a list of all the bars available. Click any one to add it to your screen. You can also click off a toolbar that you no longer need.

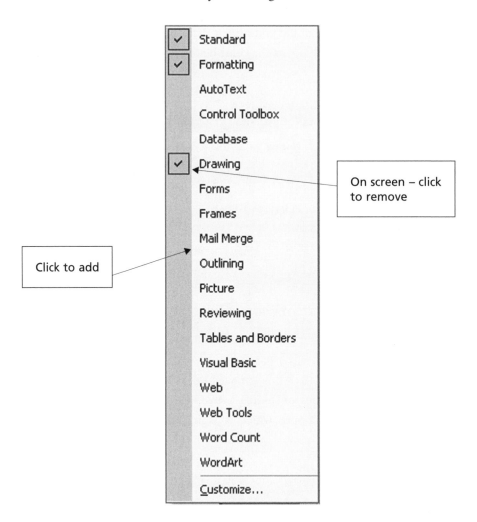

Find a missing toolbar button: For any toolbar, you can find extra toolbar buttons by clicking the down-facing arrow labelled Toolbar Options at the end of the bar, select *Add* or *Remove* buttons and then open the appropriate listing. Click any button to add or remove it from your screen display.

Each toolbar has its own range of buttons, but you can add one from another toolbar if you want to make use of it without displaying the full bar. Do this by clicking the Customize option. Under Commands, find the toolbar category containing your

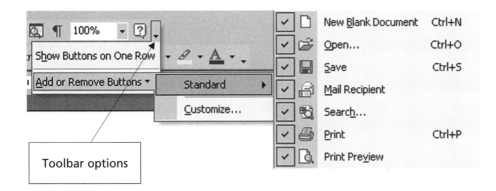

Toolbar options

chosen button in the Commands window, hold down the left mouse button, then drag the toolbar button up to your toolbar. When a black vertical line shows, let go and the button will appear. To remove a button if the bar becomes overcrowded, simply drag it off the toolbar after selecting Customize.

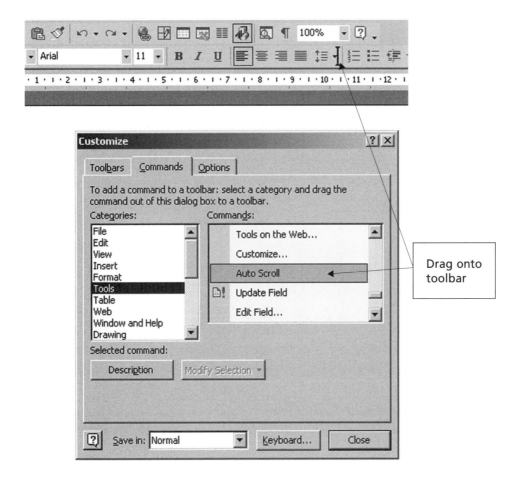

Drag onto toolbar

MISSING ITEMS

When word processing, you may find the ruler is missing, and in other applications such as *Excel* and *PowerPoint* you may want to add the Formula Bar or Grid lines if they are not showing. You may also want to add or remove the Task Pane that appears on the side of the screen offering links to parts of the system, or the temporary memory store known as the Office Clipboard if using *Windows XP*. All these items are available from the **View** or **Edit** menus – either click the tick on or off to change your screen display**.**

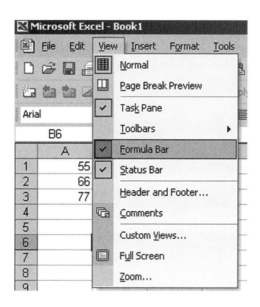

SETTING DEFAULTS

When you start working in *Word*, it can be incredibly irritating if the font type and size set by default are wrong, but when you change them they keep changing back during your typing or as soon as you start the next piece of work. Fortunately, you can set your own formats and maintain them. Do this by changing the default settings via the **Format – Font** menu. (A similar option is available from the **File – Page Setup** menu if you want to change the default margin settings.)

1. Open the **Format** menu and select **Font.**
2. Select all your preferred fonts and styles from the various boxes but, instead of clicking OK, click the *Default* button.

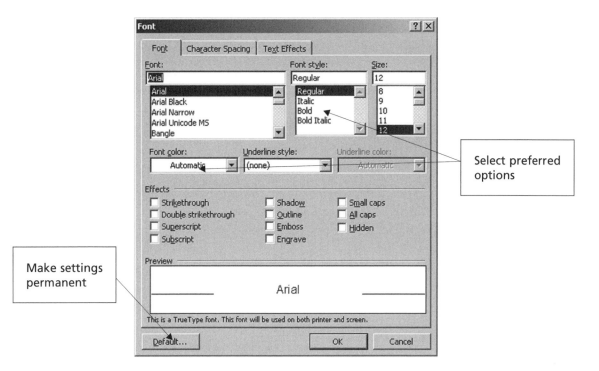

Select preferred options

Make settings permanent

3. When asked if you want future documents to take on these formats, click Yes.

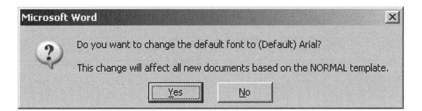

4. For the settings to take effect, you MUST start a new document. From now on, you will find your formats stay in place.

CARRY OUT A SEARCH

However carefully you save your work or install new programs, they may go missing and you need to be able to find them again. The quickest way is to use the Search facility from the **Start** menu or within folders on the desktop.

The more you know about the file or program you are looking for, the easier the search. For example:

◆ Do you know its full or partial name?
◆ Do you know the drive, folder or sub-folder in which it is stored?
◆ Do you know the date it was last modified?
◆ Do you know what type of file or program it is?

If you can answer some of these questions, your search should be very simple.

For example, imagine you want to locate any word processed files labelled *Calendar 2004*. When you open the Search box, in *Windows XP* machines you can select the type of search you want to carry out e.g. is it for pictures, programs, music or documents? Either pick a category or, if you are not sure, select the *All files and folders* option.

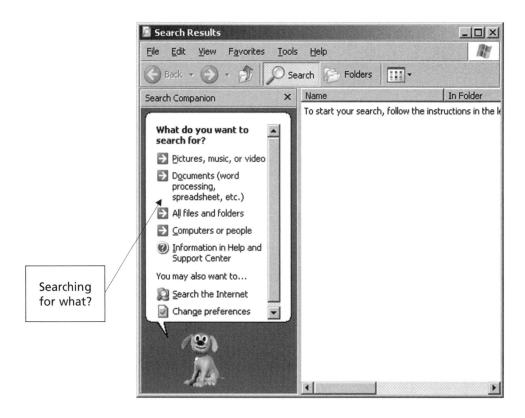

You will be offered a search box in which you can type in the file name and select the *lowest* level location you believe contains the file e.g. My Documents, a sub-folder or a floppy disk. If you don't know, select the drive you normally work on e.g. C.

Where you do not know the exact file name, use an asterix * to represent missing characters e.g. Cal*r, Calendar 200* or Calendar*. If you don't even know the name of the file or program, you could select the option to specify the date or period in which it was modified, or even type in some keywords contained in the text, but this will result in a very long search.

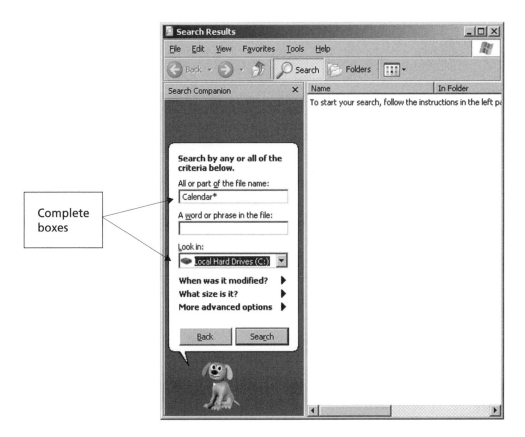

When you have completed all the boxes, click Search and the results will appear in the main window.

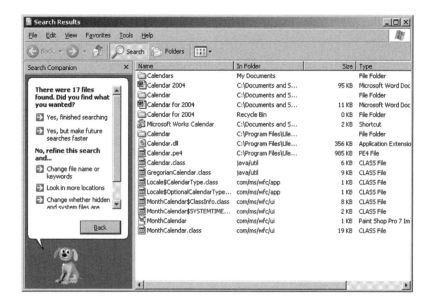

The results can be quite confusing, so if it is possible, specify the type of file you are looking for more exactly. For example, if it is a word processed document, you can add the extension **.doc** after the file name and if it is a spreadsheet, type *Calendar 2004***.xls.** For pictures, you could add **.jpg**, **.bmp** or **.gif** if you know that it is a JPEG, bitmap or GIF image (file types are covered in more detail later).

Having located the file, double-click it in the window to open it on screen.

ORGANISING THE VIEW

Most new computer users put up with the display that is offered to them, but it can sometimes be more helpful to organise the display of your files or pages differently.

Files

After a search, or when looking through a folder on the desktop, you may want to see details of a file's size or location, or change from large icons to a neat list. With pictures, you may like to view them as 'thumbnails' before opening any. You can change how files are displayed by selecting an alternative from the **View** menu.

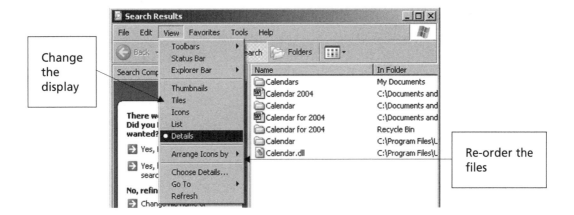

You also have a similar option from the Views button.

To change the order in which the files appear, select *Arrange Icons by* from the **View** menu and then choose to sort them by name, type, size or when last modified.

Page

Within the various applications such as *Word* and *PowerPoint*, you can view your active screen in different ways – again either choosing from the **View** menu or buttons. Page view buttons can be found in the bottom, left-hand corner of the window.

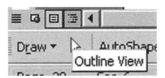

Normal view may be easier for editing, but a Print Layout view shows you how the page will look when printed, letting you work with images and other objects and check margins and spacing. Outline is useful for long documents or presentations as it allows you to restrict the view to headings and sub-headings, and the Web Layout view displays the contents as they would look on the Web. *PowerPoint* has other views related to working with slides.

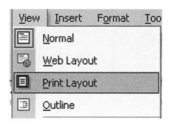

OPENING FILES

There is nothing more annoying than receiving a file by e-mail or on a disk that you cannot open. This is because, when you double-click a file, it tries to open into an application with which it is associated. If you don't have the program, you cannot open the file.

Fortunately, you can change this association to another program that you do have which may allow you to view the file.

1. Right-click the file you wish to open and select *Open with.* (Sometimes you must hold down Shift as you click to be offered this option.) You may be offered an appropriate choice of programs or you will need to select *Choose Program.*

2. When the dialog box opens, scroll down to find the best option. Click it to open the selected file or first click in the *Always . . .* checkbox so that all future files of this type are opened by the same program.

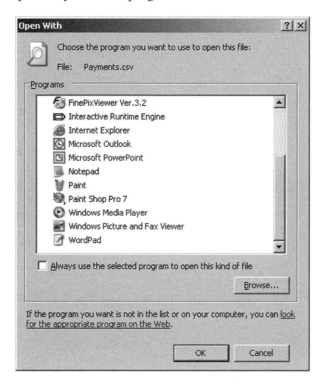

USING HELP

For some reason, computerised Help menus have a bad reputation. You should ignore this and use the help screens often; they are really quite straightforward and extremely useful if no-one is around to help sort out a problem.

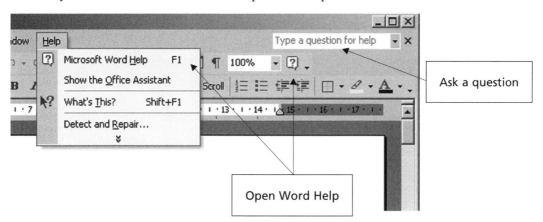

Question box

If you have a *Windows XP* machine, you will see a small box at the top of the screen in certain programs displaying the text 'Type a question for help'. This is a short-cut to the main help menu, so type your topic e.g. *changing margins,* and then press *Enter* to display a list of links to the relevant information.

Microsoft Help

Select this option from the Help menu, press the function key F1 or click the toolbar button to open the main Help window.

You will see three labelled tabs at the top left and a main display on the right.

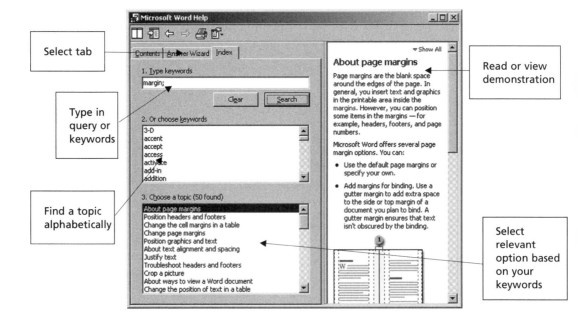

Tabs

Contents: this allows you to work down through a menu of options similar to chapter headings and sub-headings. This is useful if you want a general introduction to a major aspect of the software.

Answer wizard: like the Question box, type in a phrase or question to be shown related topics.

Index: search for topics related to a single keyword or phrase, or choose from an alphabetical list.

Office Assistant

The Clippit paperclip 'helper' used to arrive unannounced in earlier versions of Office, but you can now decide whether or not to turn it on. It works in a similar way to the question box or Answer Wizard, as well as second-guessing the help you might need when you start carrying out particular tasks. If you like to have an Assistant around but prefer a cat, dog or magician, right-click the image to choose an alternative.

What's This?

Select this option to add a question mark to your pointer ⏳**?** . Now click any toolbar button or other object and you will be offered a definition or guidance. Some dialog boxes contain a button **?** that works in the same way.

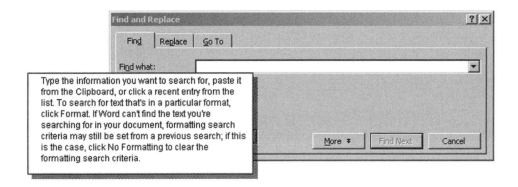

Word Processing

Depending on your job title and the business of your organisation, you may spend most of your time typing straight-forward letters and memos, or you may need to apply advanced IT skills and create complex reports, design tables or produce attractively laid-out publicity material. This chapter will show you how to carry out all the major word processing tasks you are likely to meet.

Common to many organisations is the need to make amendments to documents created by someone else who has used what might be termed 'unorthodox' methods. Changing the contents of a table, removing strange paragraph layouts or inserting an extra column of numbers is not nearly so easy if you didn't create the document in the first place; you must be able to identify what the previous author has done. This chapter ends with an introduction to strategies for detecting other people's settings.

A WORD ABOUT GRAMMAR (BUSINESS ENGLISH)

You may have excellent writing skills, but it is surprising how many people still trip up over some of the less common grammatical rules. Here is a short summary of how to deal with the awkward grammatical problems you may face.

Starting new paragraphs

If your work is criticised as being difficult to read, it may simply be because you have packed too many topics together into a single paragraph, making the text rather long-winded and indigestible.

To improve any written work, check that paragraphs are really about a single topic or field of interest, and if in doubt, start a new paragraph at a point of change. You should also think about starting new paragraphs simply to cut down on the amount of text in a single block.

Formal/informal English

Documents that will be read by anyone other than very close colleagues need to be formally written. This means that sentences should be impersonal, contain all necessary information including dates and times, avoid slang or the abbreviated form of words such as can't and won't, and, occasionally, may require a more stilted turn of phrase than usual e.g. 'unfortunately it will not be possible . . .' rather than 'sorry I can't . . .'.

E-mails have developed their own conventions, but it is an unwise person who believes it is acceptable to leave in spelling mistakes or use too informal a style when sending business e-mails. If in doubt, err on the side of formality and you won't be embarrassed.

Semi-colons

The semi-colon has two main uses – it separates out items in a complex list and it can be used to join two short sentences.

Lists: If this includes eggs, bacon, milk and ham, it is easy to read the items when separated by commas. However, what if you have a list that includes:

A large pair of men's gardening gloves
Two flowerpots decorated with ceramic mosaics
A floribunda rosebush and two clematis plants in a large planter
Several small packets of seeds including 3 varieties of bean

In the middle of a document, these items will become confusing to read unless they are separated clearly. You need to do this by using semi-colons.

The list would then read:

a large pair of men's gardening gloves; two flowerpots decorated with ceramic mosaics; a floribunda rosebush and two clematis plants in a large planter; and several small packets of seeds including 3 varieties of bean.

Linked sentences: you can use a semi-colon if you want to contrast two different statements or link related sentences.

Terry was hungry; he set out for the chip shop.

The first week was really sunny; the second week was cold and overcast.

Colons

The colon is used to introduce lists, statements or quotations. If you wonder whether to use one in a sentence, read up to the point where it might be required and, if it feels as if you are waiting for an answer, put in a colon.

We need three things from you: ....

He turned to her and said: '...

One thing is clear: ....

Apostrophes

If there is one grammatical error that crops up everywhere, it is the misuse of the apostrophe. It is *not* used for plurals e.g. *the shop sold* **videos**. There are only two places where an apostrophe is required: to show possession and to replace missing letters in a contracted word.

Possession: The rule with apostrophes is that you must concentrate on the **owner** of the object/objects, no matter how many things they own. Always put the apostrophe straight *after* the owner(s) and, if required, add an **s**.

If one book belongs to a **boy**, it is the **boy's** book

If two socks belong to a **boy**, they are the **boy's** socks

But if one book and two socks belong to *two* **boys**, they are the **boys'** book and the **boys'** socks.

If one house is shared by two **families**, it is the **families'** house

If ten dogs belong to one **family**, they are the **family's** dogs

If one school belongs to the **children**, it is the **children's** school

If twenty hats belong to five **people**, they are the **people's** hats

When a single person's name ends in **s** e.g. James, you can choose to add an extra **s** after the apostrophe or not:

James's book or **James'** book

James's hats or **James'** hats

Contraction: More familiar use of the apostrophe is to represent missing letters e.g.

cannot becomes **can't**, **will not** becomes **won't**, **shall not** becomes **shan't**, **have not** becomes **haven't** and **they are** becomes **they're**.

Do not become confused between pronouns and contractions:

Yours, **his** and **its** – these are all pronouns with *no* apostrophe e.g. the coats are **yours**, the cat is **his** and the dog lost **its** ball.

However, **it is** hot becomes **it's** hot, **you are** early becomes **you're** early and **he is** tired becomes **he's** tired.

LETTERS AND MEMOS

Even if you do not take up a secretarial post as such, you are quite likely to type your own letters and memos now and again and these will normally have to follow your organisation's stationery conventions. This section introduces some of the ways you can save time on this particular word processing task including:

◆ Templates
◆ Logos
◆ Automatic entries
◆ International characters
◆ Mail merge
◆ Envelopes and labels

Templates

In the old days, many companies used paper printed with a letterhead. However, today it would be far too tedious to replace headed paper every time a different printing job was being carried out and so the use of such paper was phased out. Instead, you will find that logos, special layouts and company addresses etc. are stored in templates. You create new documents based on these and the original stays untouched.

(Don't be tempted to create a normal document and keep re-using it for your correspondence – although you can make amendments and select Save As to save new versions, one day you will click Save by mistake and the original will be lost.)

Templates may be stored in a special folder but are commonly available from the **File – New** menu. In *Office XP* you will first be offered the Task Pane (an extra window that opens up alongside your screen offering shortcuts to various files, objects or guidance) that includes a link to General Templates, but clicking this link will open the Templates dialog box.

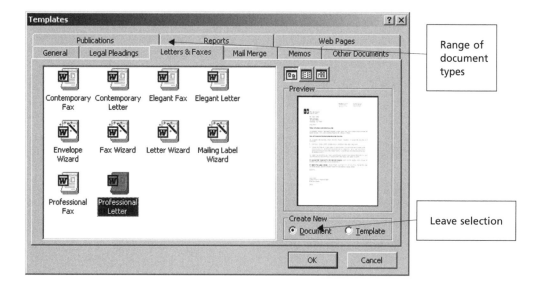

Preview the template you want to use or click the correct company letter template. Leaving the *Create New – Document* option selected means that you can treat the document that opens exactly like a normal word processed file. Make all the necessary amendments to names, dates and addresses, type the body of the letter and save as normal.

If you want to create your own customised template based on one already provided, select the *Create New – Template* option. Change the layout and any entries to be included in all future letters and then click Save. Before doing anything else, check

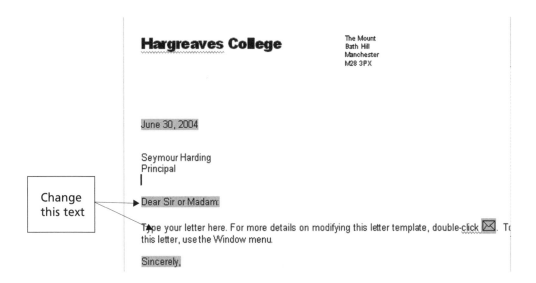

that the *Save as type*: box shows Document Template. This will open the Templates folder so that you can save your template with others in the General templates window, or you could even make a new folder to store it in.

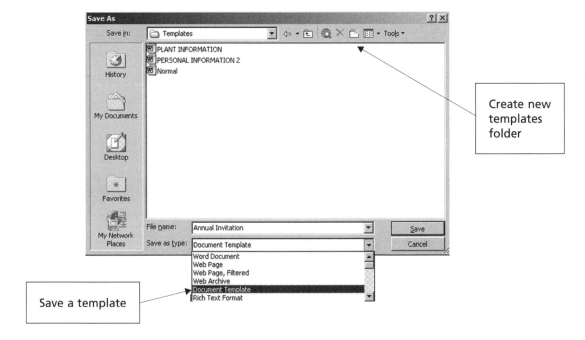

Now name the template and click *Save* and, next time you need to use it, it will be available for you on the General tab or from a new tab you have created.

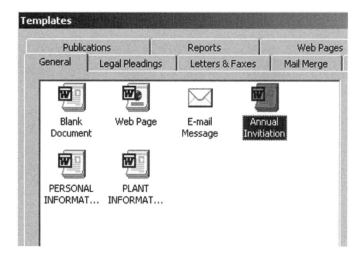

Logos and watermarks

Not everyone works in an organisation that has templates ready-prepared, and you may need to be more pro-active and prepare a set yourself. One tricky problem may be adding the company logo, and perhaps even turning it into a faded image to appear behind your text.

To add a logo, open the **Insert** menu and select **Picture – From File.** You should have been told which drive and folder contains the image, so browse through your computer until you see its name in the main window of the Insert box.

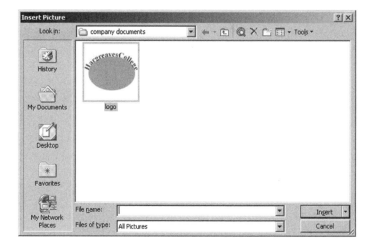

Press *Enter* or click the *Insert* button and it will appear on the page.

Resize: If the logo is too large, click to select it and show the border. Now drag one of the black squares (sizing handles) inwards when the pointer shows a 2-way arrow . U: ↔ orner sizing handle to keep the image in proportion.

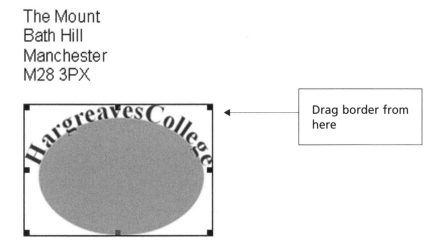

Drag border from here

Move the logo: To position the logo behind an address, (or just to move it round the page more easily) you must apply a Text wrap. This is available from the Draw menu or you can select it after right-clicking the image and choosing to show the Picture toolbar.

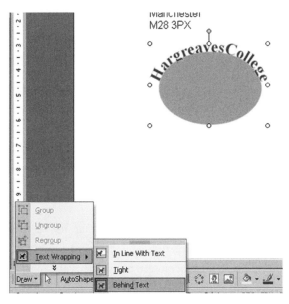

The Tight option will allow you to move the image up close to text, and Behind Text will let you position it underneath your typing. When selected, it will now show white sizing handles and, in XP, a green rotate handle. Drag the image across the page and move it into position.

One option on the Picture toolbar is to change a coloured image to black and white, greyscale or 'washout/watermark', if the image is strong enough to be visible in this format.

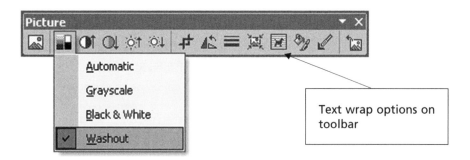

You may also be required to add a watermark to a printed document e.g. a picture such as your logo, or text e.g. *Sample* or *Confidential* that will appear centrally behind the page contents. For pictures in *Word 2000*, simply follow the above instructions but enlarge the picture so that it fills the page. Text may be more difficult but one way is to create the words as an object e.g. use *Word Art*™ (described later) or copy or create the text in the drawing package *Microsoft Paint*™ and then treat as above.

In *Office XP* you have the option from the **Format** menu. Select **Background – Printed Watermark** and then click *Picture* or *Text*. Find the picture or type your text and select horizontal or diagonal placement. View the watermark in Print Layout.

AutoText

Templates are not always time-saving as you may simply want to dash off a quick letter or memo on plain paper. Having carefully typed your address or signature details in a chosen font, layout and format, it is useful if you can recall this formatted block of text each time it is needed. One method is to save it as AutoText.

Select the text and then open the **Insert** menu and click **AutoText – New.**

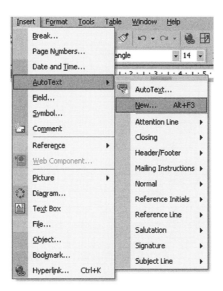

A box will appear in which you must type a short memorable codeword or phrase to identify the block of text e.g. *colladd* (standing for College address). Click *OK* and the text will be stored in your computer.

To recall it when typing your next letter, type the codeword and immediately press the Function key F3 found at the top of your keyboard.

If you ever forget your (not so) memorable phrase – don't panic. Open the Auto-Correct box by selecting **Tools – AutoCorrect Options** or go to **Insert – AutoText – AutoText.** On the AutoText tab, scroll down the list until you find the probable codeword and click it to check that it is the missing entry. You can insert it into your page from here by clicking *Insert* and will hopefully remember it next time.

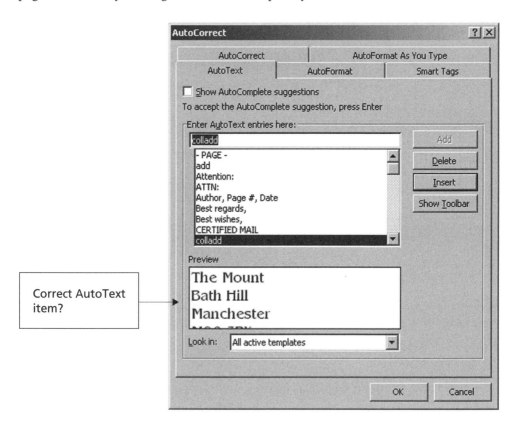

Correct AutoText item?

If you have made an error with the original block of text, you can overwrite the AutoText entry quite easily. Simply type out the text correctly, repeat setup using the original abbreviation and press Enter. When asked if you want to update the original, click *Yes*.

Automatic corrections

You may find that the machine sometimes reads your mind wrongly and carries out unwanted actions. For example, if you type 1/2 it may turn this into ½ when you didn't want a fraction, e-mail addresses may become blue and underlined when you prefer them to remain simple text and, if you type 1st, it changes to 1st.

There are two methods for turning off these corrections – either backspace and you may find your typing returns to its original form, or open the **Tools** menu, select **AutoCorrect Options** and click the *AutoFormat As You Type* tab. Take off the tick against any automatic feature you don't want and then click OK.

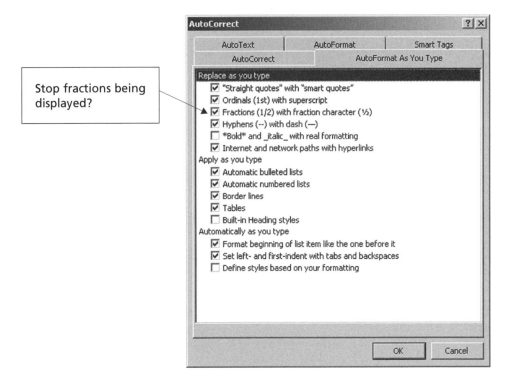

Stop fractions being displayed?

Other changes may take place such as a typing error being corrected automatically, a smiley face appearing ☺ when you type a colon and then close brackets :), or two dashes — and > becoming →. These replacements are listed on the *AutoCorrect* tab.

To add a new Auto Correction, type your chosen abbreviation, symbols or misspelled word in the Replace: box and the new word or symbol you want displayed in the With: box before clicking *Add*. The replacement will now take place automatically as you type.

Remove unwanted replacements by selecting them from the list in the window and clicking *Delete*.

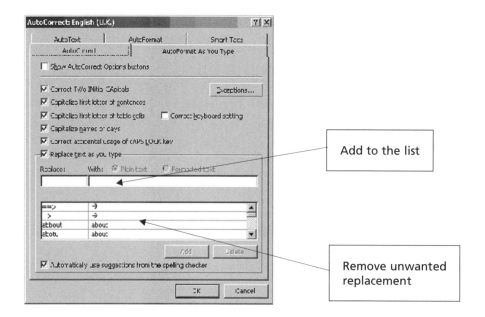

Unwanted capital letters

As it is so easy to leave the Caps Lock on and not notice until you have typed a large block of text in capital letters, one trick worth remembering is how to change text from capitals back to normal type. Simply select the block of text, hold down Shift and press the function key F3. This toggles through all upper case, all lower case and Initial capitals. Further options are available from the **Format – Change Case** menu.

Dates

Don't waste time typing dates. To add one to letters, select *Date and Time* from the **Insert** menu and choose your preferred format. One option is to click the checkbox that will mean the date is always updated in your letter. This is useful if you are delaying printing but want the accurate date on your correspondence. The downside is that, if you check your saved letter later, it will always show the current date, *not* the date you wrote it.

International characters

When writing to foreign customers, clients or colleagues, it is very professional if you can add the correct accent e.g. the umlaut for Zoë or acute over the e in José. Although there is always the Insert – Symbol box in XP machines, for older operating systems you can add some accents using the keyboard.

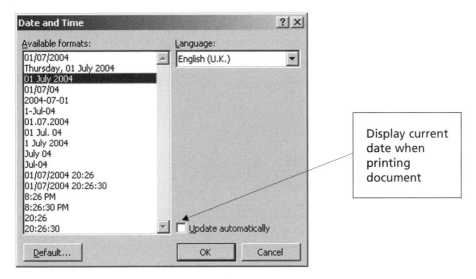

1. Find the appropriate symbol on the keys: colon for umlaut ü, apostrophe for acute é, comma for cedilla ç and the ¬ key to the left of 1 for grave é etc.
2. Type the symbol by holding down Ctrl and then pressing the key (for a symbol on the lower part of a key), or holding Ctrl plus Shift (for an upper symbol). Nothing will appear on the page.
3. Now type the letter and the symbol will appear over it.

Mail merge

One job that computers have made almost pleasant is sending the same, personalised letter, invoice or reminder to a large number of people.

You are likely to work in an organisation where extensive databases of client, customer or staff records are already held in the system and you will want to use these names and addresses for your mailing list. This information is known as the *data source*. Mailing list details can be in any recognisable form though they are commonly *Excel* spreadsheets or *Access* databases. However, you can also create a data source from within *Word* using the 'helper' (a wizard) if you need to set up a small mailing list from scratch, or even type a simple table and use that. The important requirement is that each column has a heading (field name) describing the information it contains.

First Name	*Surname*	*Salary*	*Department*
John	Haynes	£23,000	Finance
Peter	Mackay	£45,000	Planning
Heidi	Tims	£32,500	Human Resources

Mail merge allows you to link a data source with your word processed letter – the *main document* – and then merge the two together. In *Office XP* you will be given far more guidance on setting up the mail merge than in *Word 2000*, and must start the process by clicking **Tools – Letters and Mailings – Mail Merge Wizard.** There are 6 steps to take that guide you through the process.

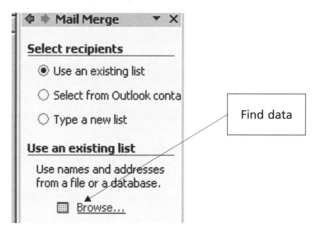

If you are ready with a letter template or blank page, choose to create a letter using the current document and then select the recipients using an existing list.

Browse through your files until you locate the data source you want to use and select the correct sheet or table before clicking OK. If you need to, filter out any unwanted records first. Each field will have an arrow next to its name that you click to display all the entries. Select one for a perfect match or click (Advanced) and use the Filter and Sort options to set filter criteria.

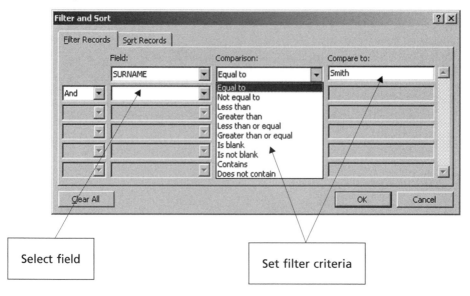

You can now write your letter and, whenever you need to add a name or address, click the link to *More items*.

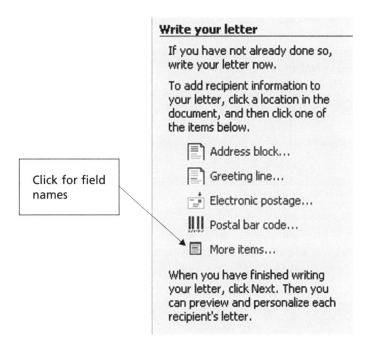

Click for field names

This opens up a window showing the field names in your data source, and each time you come to a relevant point in your letter, select and insert the appropriate field name.

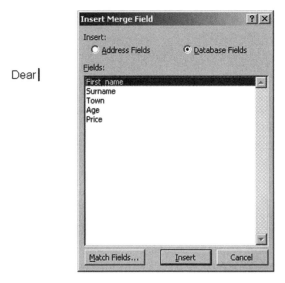

Continue writing until you have completed your letter. The fields will be clearly distinguishable from the rest of the text.

> Dear «First_name»
>
> I hope, now you have come to stay in «Town» that you find the climate suits you. Now you are «Age», entrance to the museum will only cost «Price» for an annual season ticket.
>
> Buy yours soon as there are a limited number available.
>
> Yours sincerely
>
> Charles Crawley
> Curator

To preview the letters with actual names and details drawn from your data source in place, move on to Step 5 and you will see the relevant information extracted from the first record. Click the arrows to move through your records to view further letters.

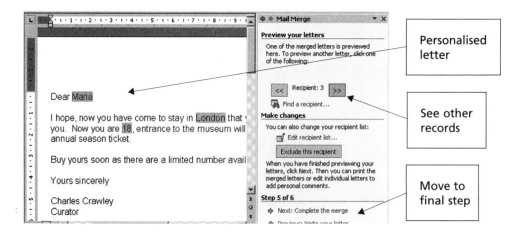

The final step involves printing all or selected letters or, by clicking *Edit individual letters,* creating a new file containing the merged letters set out one to a page. This format is more transportable and may be useful if, for example, you needed to take the letters on a floppy disk to a different machine and would not have room for the full database.

Do not forget to save the main document or data source before closing *Word* if you have not already done so. They will be linked each time the main document is opened if they are still on the same network.

At the very start of the process, if you create e-mail messages rather than letters, you can carry out a mail merge for e-mails as long as one of your fields includes the full e-mail address of all your recipients. When you reach the printing stage, you will be offered a window in which to add the e-mail address field to your To: box and can then send your messages to everyone in your database.

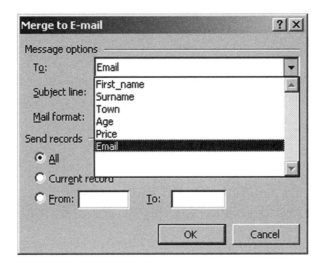

In *Word 2000*, the wizard looks slightly different, although the process is just the same.

1. Open the letter you want to send, or start a new one using a blank document or template, go to the **Tools** menu and select **Mail Merge.**
2. In Step 1 click *Create* to set up the main document and choose *Form Letters* as this term covers everything except labels and envelopes. To stay with the document you have opened, select *Active Window* and then move on to the next step.
3. Step 2 is where you locate the data source. Click *Data Source – Get Data* and choose the option to *Open* a database already stored on your system. You must now browse through the files, looking for the appropriate types of file, until you locate the correct database. If necessary, select a specific spreadsheet or table of data.

4. You are now ready to return to your letter to add the personal details. Select *Edit Main Document* and you will see a new toolbar has appeared across the top of the screen. This is also available in *Word 2002* from the **Tools** menu if you prefer it to the wizard.

5. At every point in your letter, insert the correct field name by clicking the Insert Merge Field button and selecting from the list. The letter will appear with fieldnames in place.

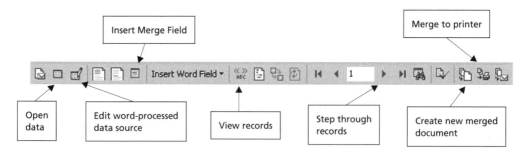

6. To view actual records, click the <<ABC>> button on the toolbar, and use the arrows to move backwards and forwards through the letters.
7. There is a shortcut on the toolbar for printing all your letters, as well as one to a new, merged file if you prefer to save the merged letters separately.
8. Save the main document before closing, so that it can be used again in the future. It will remain linked to the data source as long as both files remain on the computer.
9. To select a sub-set of records to merge to, you will need to return to the Mail Merge wizard and select the Query Options in Step 3.

Labels and envelopes

The mail merge process is also used for creating labels or envelopes based on a mailing list. At step 1, you must select the appropriate object to create i.e. envelopes or labels and then use the next step to set up the correct layout and size. Now continue through the steps in exactly the same way as for a letters mail merge to open the appropriate database and insert the fields into your label or envelope before printing.

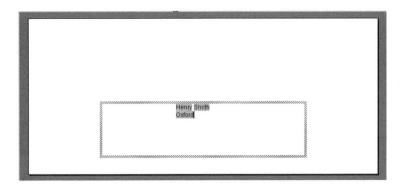

MINUTES OF MEETINGS

Minutes are notoriously difficult to type. This is due to the constant numbering changes they usually incorporate. However, if you bear in mind that this is just about 'levels' of text, it may make controlling the numbers easier. In *Word* this is known as outline numbering.

1. Discussion of site for new annexe
    a. Report from architect
    b. Financial position
        i. Funding
        ii. Forecast
    c. Environmental considerations

2. Sponsorship
    a. Present position
    b. New contacts
        i. Report from Marketing manager
        ii. Presentation by Peter's team

Creating numbered lists

To create the top level text – numbers 1 and 2 in the example, you can click on the Numbering button 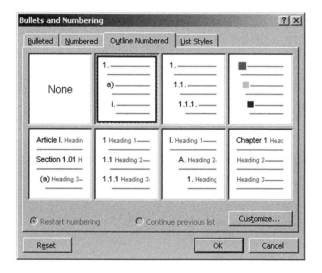 on the toolbar. Every time you press Enter, the next number will appear.

To create the entries numbered a, b, c, press Enter so that you are on the next line and *then* press the tab key (left of Q). This takes you *down* a level and now each time you press Enter you will remain at this level until you want to change.

To go down to a further level – i, ii etc, simply press Enter and then the tab key. To go back *up* one or more levels, hold Shift as you press tab and the direction is reversed.

Unnumbered lines: If you want to add extra text on a new line that is not a continuation of the numbering, hold Shift as you press *Enter.* You may have to sort out the indentation from the margin but can then type your text before pressing Enter and continuing with the numbering again. (Alternatively, complete the list with numbers and then click any line and turn off the toolbar button to remove the numbers from that particular part of the list.)

Settings: In many machines, the numbers do not appear automatically. To set these, you must turn on Outline Numbering manually. Do this by opening the **Format** menu and selecting **Bullets and Numbering**.

Click the *Outline Numbered* tab and select your preferred style of numbering.

You may decide that, rather than a, b, c etc. you prefer to see a) b) or even A) B). Change the style of any level of numbers by clicking the Customize button. For any level, select it in the list and then choose a Number style. You can change the font or even type into the Number format: box to remove brackets or add full stops etc. if your exact style is not offered. You can also change the spacing for text or numbers on the page. When you have customised all the levels, click *OK*.

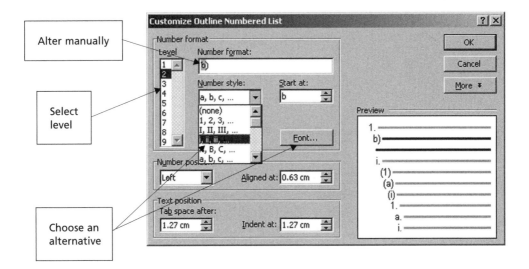

LONG DOCUMENTS

When you are required to type anything longer than two or three pages, there are a number of techniques that can be applied. Not only will they make your document easier to read but they will also help you manage the process more effectively.

This section covers:

- ◆ Spelling
- ◆ Page numbers
- ◆ Headers and footers
- ◆ Moving text
- ◆ Replacing entries
- ◆ Importing objects
- ◆ Styles and table of contents
- ◆ Indexing
- ◆ Sharing documents

Spelling

As you type, spelling mistakes or grammatical errors are highlighted with red or green lines. Rather than run the spell checker on the whole document, deal with these words as they appear by right-clicking the line and selecting one of the options e.g. replace the word, ignore it, correct it automatically in future or add it to the dictionary.

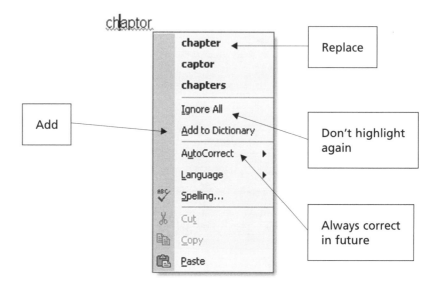

Page numbers

A quick way to add numbers is to insert them from the **Insert** menu. Select the position on the page where numbers will appear, and click the box if you do not want the first page numbered.

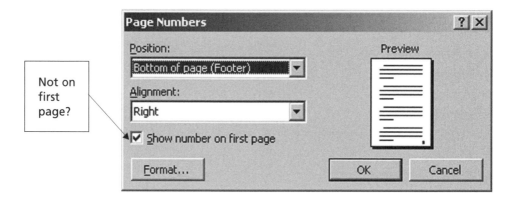

Headers and footers

To add extra information on each page, you may prefer to work with headers and footers. Including page numbers, these are any entries added in the top or bottom margins that do not interfere with page content.

Select the option from the **View** menu. In the box that appears, either type your text e.g. a chapter heading or your name, or select an option such as an automatic date, time or page number from the toolbar. Move across the header box to add extra entries by double-clicking your mouse or pressing the tab key, and add entries on a new line by pressing *Enter*. Click the *Switch Between* button if you want to add entries in the bottom margin, and then return to your document by clicking the *Close* button or double-clicking the document text that will be visible but faded.

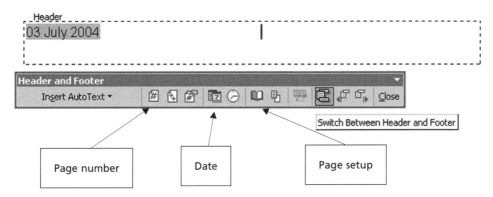

If required, select a ready-prepared entry from the Insert AutoText box. These include the filename and path, to display the folder location of your document, and a 'page 5 of 17' type entry which will be updated as you add further pages.

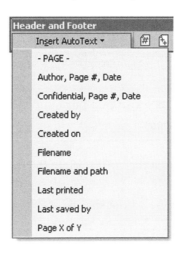

For many long documents, you won't want the header or footer to show on the first page. Click the *Page Setup* button to open the dialog box and place a tick in the checkbox.

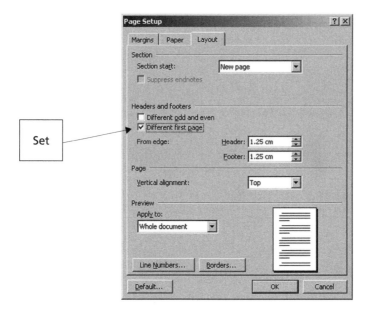

You will now find that your first page offers an empty header box labelled differently in which you can type a unique header or can simply leave blank.

First Page Header

Move text (Cut and Paste)

In case you have forgotten, there is a simple way to move a block of text if you decide it is in the wrong position. Carry out the move in 4 steps:

1. Select the text to move

2. Click Cut (right-click the block to find this option, click the toolbar button or select from the **Edit** menu)

3. Click on the page to position the cursor where the text is to go

4. Click Paste and then sort out spacing and formats.

If you want the original text to remain in place but add a copy of it somewhere else, click Copy   at step 2.

You may want to copy or cut several items. Later versions of *Word* have increased the number of items you can retain in the computer's memory – the Clipboard – and you may find that this opens to allow you to select an item to Paste. In *Word 2002* you can open the Office Clipboard from the **Edit** menu.

If you want to move text a short distance, you can also select it and then drag it into place with the mouse. However, this can be tricky across pages or with large blocks of text so choose Cut and Paste as a more controllable method.

Selecting a large block of text

It is quite common to need to select a block of text that is too long to view and that therefore extends below the screen. Dragging the mouse to select it can prove very difficult, so carry out the selection as follows: click in front of the first word, scroll down to the end using the scroll bar and then hold Shift as you click your mouse after the last word. The complete block will now be selected.

Find or replace text

Having written a 20 page report, it is annoying to discover suddenly that you have typed Mrs *Hard* instead of Mrs *Hand* all the way through. To replace the word wherever it appears, open the **Edit** menu and select **Replace.** In the Find what: box type your mis-spelt word, and in the Replace with: box type the correct name. As the

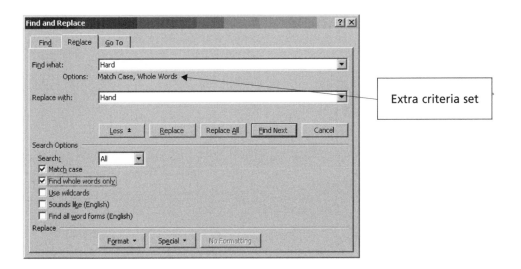

words *hard, hardly* and *hardiness* may also be present in the document, you won't want every occurrence to be changed to *hand,* so click the More/Less button to open the lower part of the window. You can now select options such as replacing whole words only and matching upper and lower case letters, to make sure only *Hard* is replaced.

If you are now sure the replacement will be acceptable, click the *Replace All* button. If in doubt, click *Find Next* to display the first matching entry and then click *Replace.* Keep doing this, clicking *Find Next* if you come to a word that you want to leave in the document. **Edit – Replace** is particularly useful if you need to type a long, complicated word several times. Use an abbreviation in the report and then replace all these entries in one go when the document is complete. Use **Edit – Find** to locate a particular word in your document – again, click *Find Next* to move on to the next occurrence.

Page and section breaks

Long documents are often divided into different chapters or sections. To make sure each of these begins on a new page, you will need to insert a page or section break. These entries then won't be affected by extra text added earlier in the document.

Page breaks are enough if you simply want to ensure the first words start on a new page, but use a section break if you need to maintain distinct formats e.g. you may need to type a different header or footer, or change the page orientation when displaying an imported picture or spreadsheet more clearly.

1. Click at the beginning of the word that will start on the new page. A shortcut to a page break is to hold Ctrl and press the Enter key.

2. Alternatively, open the **Insert** menu and select **Break.** Select either Page or Section break and decide whether this should start on the next page or not.

3. You may add a break by mistake. If you turn on the Show/Hide  button, you will see the break as a dotted line, so delete it by clicking the line and pressing Delete.

··Page Break··

Import files and objects

Long documents are often made up of files or include objects created using other software applications e.g. database tables, spreadsheets, charts or drawings. Depending on the item, you may want to import a text file, object or picture. All can be brought in relatively easily from the **Insert** menu.

Go to **Insert – File** when you want to add a text file. However, if you use this option for pictures you will end up with gobbledygook as *Word* will not be able to interpret the contents.

```
-„WAŞZ_ÞÚĨuib.a☐wJC/Ĕ=HëX×´¬´☐☐☐ô¥Ĩ-‡k+▪³Njm+v¦!☐^Úv‡_»÷0Ö¨V…œ¶¦>Lÿ☐17
"`Ÿ,0… ·£ç·0‹☐☐Äe☐sŽ{Uz´Y7ôéQÐĖÕ±„ĖhNÂFìṗ°ˢ¡Â☐Ã±\WGáK̄;k☐☐4…U„Ï´☐
```

For images such as photos or drawings, use the **Insert – Picture – from File** option. You should be able to preview any pictures before inserting them.

Add to page

For everything other than pictures e.g. charts, spreadsheets or database tables, go to **Insert – Object** and select Create from File. Click the *Browse* button to search for the target file, select it to add its name to the File name: box and click *OK*.

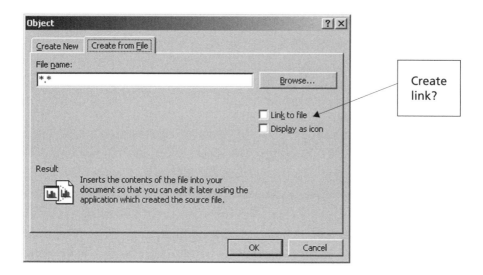

If you are going to work further on the spreadsheet, chart or database and always want the latest version displayed in your word processed document, click the *Link to file:* checkbox. Every time you re-open *Word*, you will be able to update the document with the latest version of your object.

As well as changing their size and position, objects added from the **Insert** menu (rather than copied and pasted into your document) can be edited fully: double click them and toolbars and scroll bars will appear to enable you to make your changes. With an *Excel* file, you can also change the display by moving to another sheet. Click on a blank part of the page to deselect the object once you have completed your amendments.

	A	B	C	D
1	Item	Quanity	Unit Cost	Price
2	Sheets	10	£3.50	35
3	Bedspreads	3	£8.75	26.25
4	Duvets	7	£12.00	84
5	Pillowcases	8	£3.99	31.92
6	Towels (Large)	11	£4.50	49.5

Click to display contents of different sheet instead?

Styles

Next to the Font box on the toolbar, you will see another box that will probably display the word Normal. If you click the drop-down arrow in the box, you will be offered a range of styles that can be applied to your document. So, for example, if you want a heading to be bold, italic, Arial size 14, you can format your selected text to this straight away by applying Heading 2.

Although there are a number of ready-made styles, you can easily make your own.

1. Make sure Normal is showing in the style box.
2. Type some text and then apply your chosen formats to fonts or paragraph settings.
3. With your text selected, click the word Normal or, in *2002* the description that appears in the style box, to turn it blue and then type over it the name for your new style e.g. *My Chapter Title* and press Enter.
4. This new style will now be available for you to apply throughout your document.

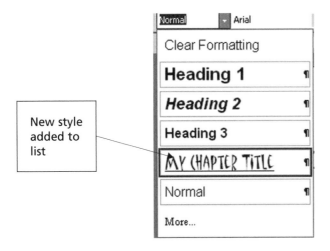

New style added to list

Again in *2002*, you may prefer to click the Styles and Formatting button 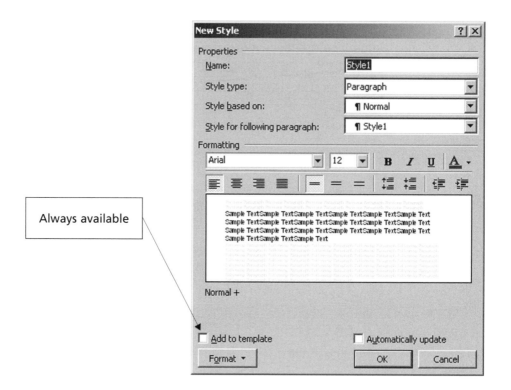 next to the Style box and, in the Task Pane that appears, click *New Style*. A dialog box opens and you can select your formatting options here, name the style and click *OK* to add it to the list. For it to be available wherever you are in *Word*, select the option to add it to the style templates.

Always available

Table of contents

Styles are particularly useful if your report, booklet or manual needs a table of contents. As long as your document includes at least two different styles, create one as follows:

1. Click in position for the table of contents – usually it is found on the first page of a document and you can first type in your headings e.g. *Contents* and *Page numbers*.
2. Go to **Insert – Index and Tables** (in 2002 you first select **Reference**) and click the *Table of Contents* tab.
3. Unless you have applied your own styles, you can leave the computer to pick up the top three levels of heading and simply select a design from the Formats box and click *OK*.

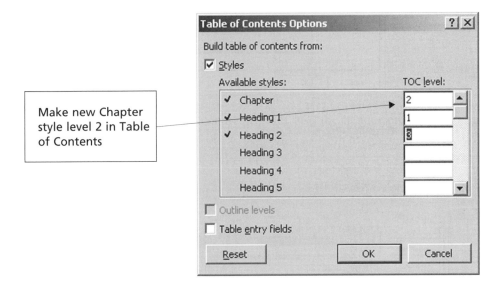

4. Where you have used your own style, click the *Options* button and make sure the name is included at the appropriate level.

Make new Chapter style level 2 in Table of Contents

5. To update the table as you make changes to your document, click in the block of text and press function key F9 or right-click and select *Update*.

Format Painter

Styles are useful if you regularly use certain formats, but sometimes you will change the look of a line or block of text once and may then want to repeat this formatting further down the page but not go through the process of creating and naming a new style.

Select the formatted text and then click the *Format Painter* button 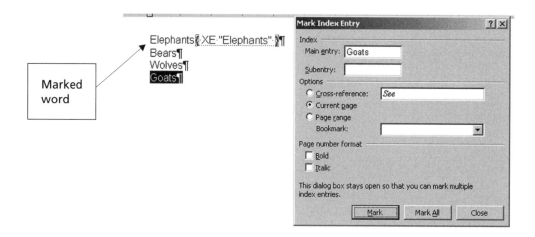 . As you move your mouse, the pointer will now show a brush. Click and drag to sweep the brush pointer across any text and it will take on the new formatting.

To repeat this action several times, double click the button first of all to keep it turned on. When you have completed all your amendments, click the button again to turn it off.

Index

Although less common in office documents, you may want an index of words at the back of a long document to help people move quickly to the appropriate page. To create an index, you must mark the words that will be included and then create an index based on these marked words.

1. Select the first word(s) to mark and hold down Alt and Shift as you then press X.
2. This opens the marking dialog box. Your index entry will be visible in the Main entry box – change the wording if necessary and then click *Mark*.
3. You will now see all keystrokes that have been used to create your document and the marked words will display their index entry inside brackets {XE 'word'}.

4. The marking box stays open so click on the page to return to your document and scroll down to the next word. Repeat the marking until all words have been marked.

5. Click where you want your index – usually on a new page at the end of the document – and add a title if you want one. Now go to **Insert – (Reference) – Index and Tables** and click the *Index tab*.

6. Choose a style of index and click *OK*.

7. To update the index if you add new pages or want to mark extra words, click an entry and press function key F9 or right-click and select *Update*.

Sharing documents

It is quite common for several people to work on the same documents, and so *Word* allows you to track changes that have been made.

1. Open the **Tools** menu and select **Track changes.** This adds the Reviewing toolbar to the screen.

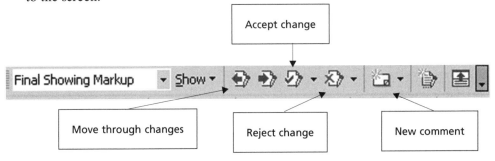

2. As you work on a document, your amendments will be highlighted and annotated in the margin. When you receive an amended document, hover over any coloured text in the document with your mouse if you want to see details of the author who changed that particular part.

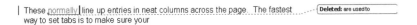

3. If you don't want to make a change but simply highlight something for the next author to follow up, double click a word and then click the *New Comment* toolbar button or go to **Insert – Comment.** A new balloon will appear in which you can type your comment. If you receive a document including comments, you can type into the balloon with your answer.

itries in neat columns across the page. The fastest ·····| **Deleted:** are used to

sure your ⎯⎯⎯⎯⎯⎯⎯⎯⎯⎯⎯⎯⎯⎯⎯⎯| **Comment:** Certain?

4. To revert to an earlier version of an amendment, select the coloured text and click the *Reject Change* button.

5. To save different versions of a document, open the **File** menu each time and select **Versions.** The history of earlier saves will be visible. Click *Save Now* to add your comments in the box that will appear and click the checkbox if you want to save new versions every time you close the document.

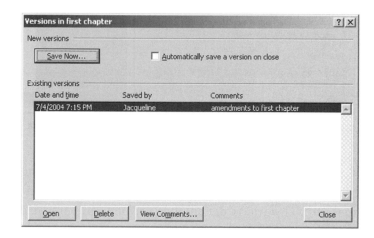

TABS

These are used to line up entries in neat columns across the page. The quick way to set tabs is to make sure your cursor is ready on the left (after typing column headings which are easier to adjust if *not* entered using a tab) and then click on the ruler, just below the markings, wherever you want your columns to start. You won't need to set a tab for the first column if this begins at the left margin.

If you don't want initial characters in every column to line up, select a different tab style from the default Left tab by clicking the button on the left of the ruler until your choice is displayed:

   Left tab – initial characters line up on the left

   Centre tab – entries are centred down the column

Right tab – last characters line up on the right

Decimal tab – decimal points line up for numerical entries

Once tabs are set, type the first entry and then press the tab key (left of Q) once. This will jump directly to the position for typing the second column. Repeat across the page and then press Enter to start entering your next line of entries.

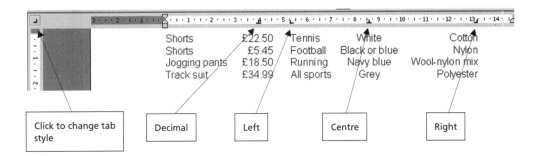

Amendments

Remove a tab: Click on the unwanted symbol, hold down the mouse button and then gently drag the tab off the ruler. When you let go, it will disappear.

Move tab positions: When columns have been set using tabs, you often find you have set them too close or need to add a new line where entries are too long and interfere with those in a separate column. It is extremely easy to get yourself in a tangle over tabs as most people make the mistake of changing the tab stop position for the problem line only.

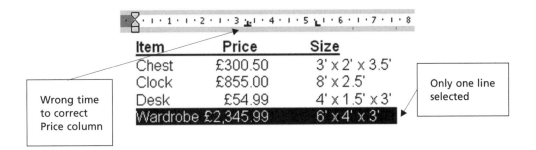

Now the whole set of data becomes impossible to work with as different tab stops apply to different entries.

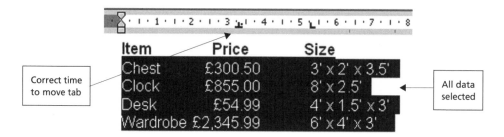

Fortunately, you should have no trouble if you follow the golden rule:

Always select every line that has been typed using the tabs before making changes.

If you do this, you can easily drag tabs along to a new position to accommodate extra-long entries as the changes will always apply to the whole column.

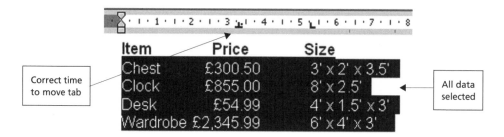

TABLES

Tables are an alternative way to display columns but are also commonly used for forms, invoices or timetables.

Create a table

To create a simple table, click on the page in the correct position for the table and then click the Insert Table button and drag your mouse across the number of columns and rows you think you will need. When you let go, the table will appear.

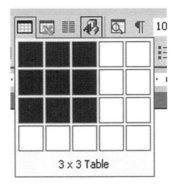

It is likely that, on occasion, you will need a more complex table design. Draw your own by opening the **Table** menu and selecting **Draw Table.** Your pointer will now display a pen and you can sketch out your preferred layout.

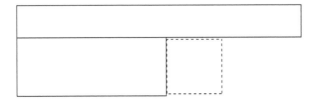

Edit a table

It is easy to increase or decrease column widths and row heights simply by dragging a square (cell) border – your mouse over any edge will show a 2-way arrow. However, it is a good idea to find the column boundary on the ruler and drag from here, rather than within the table. You won't then change a single cell dimension in the middle of a column.

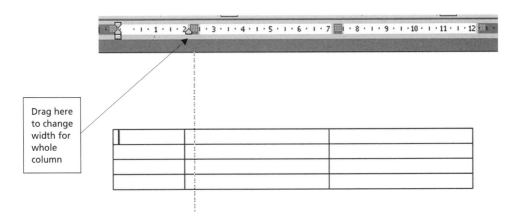

Drag here to change width for whole column

You can also open the **Table** menu, select **Table Properties** and set the size for the whole table, alignments within cells or column widths more exactly.

If you find you need extra rows at the bottom of a table, click in the last cell and press the tab key. You can also insert rows or columns anywhere by clicking a neighbouring cell and then opening the **Table** menu and selecting an **Insert** option.

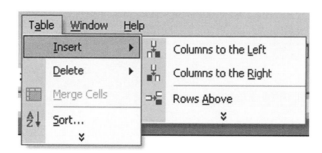

When you click in a table, a small square will appear in the top, left hand corner. Click this to select the whole table or click and drag the square to move the table across the page.

To delete a table, select it and then go to **Table – Delete Table** to remove it completely from the page. Pressing the Delete key will only remove cell *entries* in a selected table and leave empty cells.

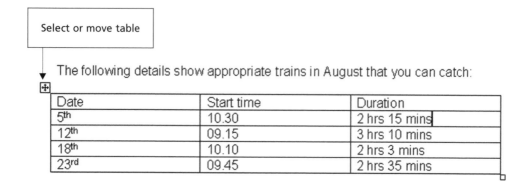

To customise a standard table, perhaps to create clear headings etc. you can merge selected cells together and then centre the contents.

August Train Times	
Date	Start time
5th	10.30
12th	09.15
18th	10.10
23rd	09.45

Table formats

Without gridlines, tables can be an easier way to display columns of text and numbers than using tabs. This is because amending an entry in one cell does not affect neighbouring columns in the same way. Keeping gridlines and adding shading and borders on the other hand can make headings or data stand out very effectively.

To remove the gridlines, select *None* from the Borders tab in the **Format – Borders and Shading** menu. To add effects, select the columns or rows and then add a boxed border or grid setting and colour the cells from the Shading tab.

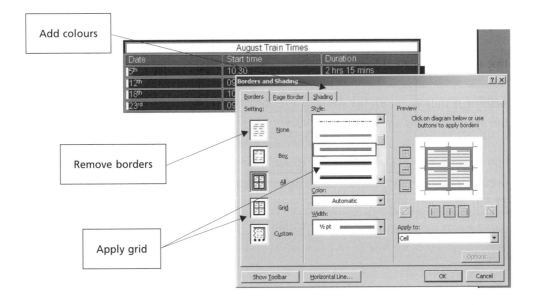

To change the look of a table quickly, open the **Table** menu and select **Table AutoFormat.** You can now choose a complete design to apply.

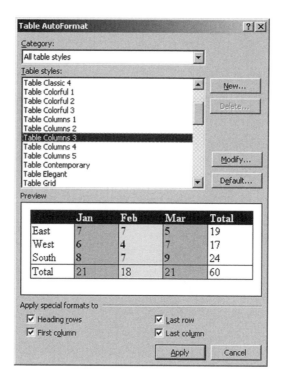

Sorting

With a large table, you may like to display the information it contains in alphabetic order or from highest to lowest price etc. To sort the entries, it is easier if you select the *headings* as well as table contents as these will be labelled properly, rather than show as Column 1, 2, 3 etc. when you select options from the dialog box. Now go to **Table – Sort** and check the Header row box to remove them from the re-ordering process. Select the appropriate column in the Sort by box and make sure entries will be displayed in the correct order. You can select three levels of sort if preferred e.g. first by date, then by time and then by duration.

Calculations in tables

For invoices and other financial tables, you can include formulae to total, average or multiply your figures. To do this, each cell must contain a distinct numerical value.

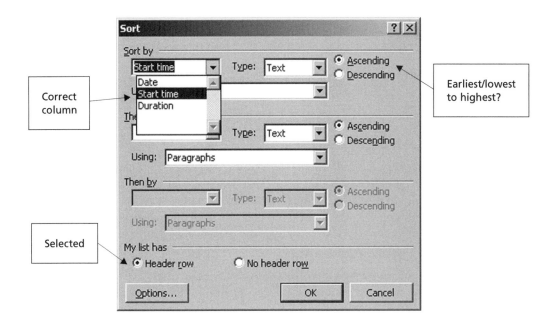

Click the cell where you want the result to appear and then open the **Table** menu and select **Formula.** A dialog box will open with a formula for totalling your column already in place. If this is the wrong formula, amend the entry manually. Although columns and rows do not display letters or numbers, the first cell in the table is A1 and alternative formulae can be written exactly as in a spreadsheet application e.g. =AVERAGE(B2:B6). (See Chapter 4 for help on formulae.)

The answer will appear against a shaded background.

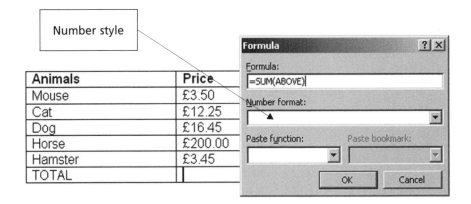

If you change any entries, update the total by right-clicking the cell and selecting *Update Field*.

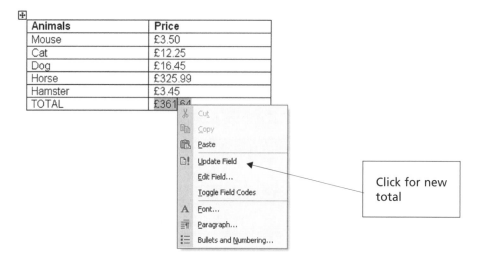

Changing text to tables

A final, useful facility offered by *Word* is to change text into tables and vice versa. This is particularly important if you want to copy data from a word processed document into a spreadsheet. As long as the entries are separated by simple spaces or tabs, select the block of text and go to **Table – Convert – Text to Table**. Set the number of columns and, if not showing, click in Other and press the appropriate key for the type of separator.

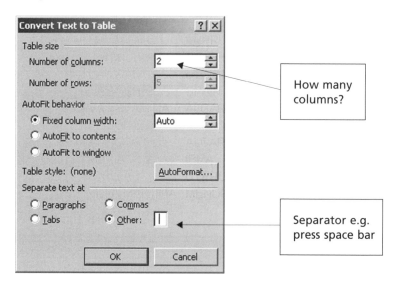

When the table appears, copy the data across to a spreadsheet as follows: select the data, click *Copy* and then move to your spreadsheet application. Click *one* cell and select *Paste*.

PUBLICITY MATERIAL

At some stage, you are quite likely to be asked to produce a leaflet, advertisement, poster or other publication. Later in this book you will find out how to use the dedicated desktop publishing (DTP) package *Publisher*, but it is quite possible to create publications using the facilities in *Word*.

Useful items to include:

◆ Appropriate text types
◆ Dropped capitals
◆ Pictures
◆ Borders
◆ Columns
◆ Word Art

Text types
Some text is easier to read than others:

This has been written in Rockwell Extra Bold 14
This has been written in Courier New 14
This has been written in Comic Sans 14
THiS HAS BEEN WRiTTEN iN MATiSSE iTC 14

Selecting the appropriate font is important, and as well as the look of individual fonts there are three main font 'families' to consider: <u>script</u> that looks rather like handwriting; <u>serif</u> where the letters have little extra lines at the ends e.g. Times New Roman; and <u>sans serif</u> fonts such as Arial that are plain in style. Experiment with fonts as you may find some are more effective than others for headings or main text.

Dropped capitals

To start each paragraph or page with a flourish, you may like to add a dropped capital.

> # T
> he house and garde
> 10.30 am – 3.00 pm
> scones will be serve

1. Click the first word and go to **Format – Drop Cap.**
2. In the dialog box, select a font type and letter position, set the size in terms of number of dropped lines and then click *OK*.

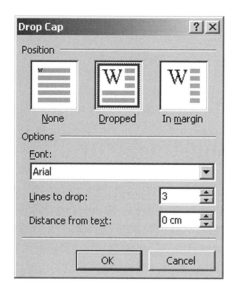

Pictures

There are three sources of picture you can add to a word processed document: the clip art gallery provided with most *Office* applications; any image files saved onto your computer or on a disk; and pictures or photos copied directly e.g. from the World Wide Web, camera, scanner or drawing package such as *Paint*.

Insert Clip Art
1. Click the Insert Clip Art button on the Drawing toolbar. In *Word 2002* you will be offered the task pane, but a gallery will open in *Word 2000*.

2. Type a subject into the box and press *Enter* or click the *Search* button. With *Word 2000*, you can also click a category heading and view related pictures.

3. When images appear in *2002*, scroll down and click any one to add it to your document. If you do not like any of them, click the *Modify* button to start a new search. You may need to insert the *Microsoft Office* CD-ROM to provide pictures that have not been installed.

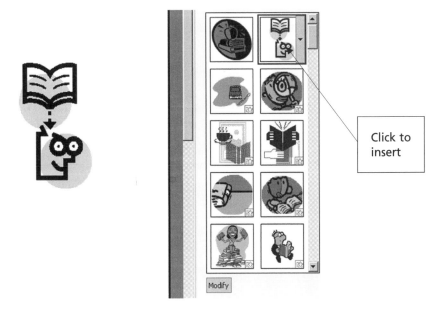

Click to insert

4. In earlier versions of *Word*, after selecting the image you need to click the top, *Insert Clip* button and then close the gallery.

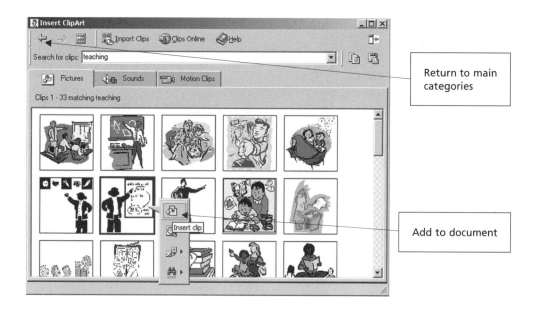

5. Once on the page, the selected picture will have a black border. Resize it by dragging a corner box – to preserve proportions – when the pointer shows a 2-way arrow.

6. Re-align a picture by using the normal alignment buttons. To be able to move the picture round more easily, open the Draw menu or right-click the picture to click *Show Picture Toolbar* and select **Text Wrapping – Tight**. The black sizing handles will become white and you can now drag the picture into position. In *2002* you will also have a green circle on a rotating arm – drag this with the mouse to rotate the picture.

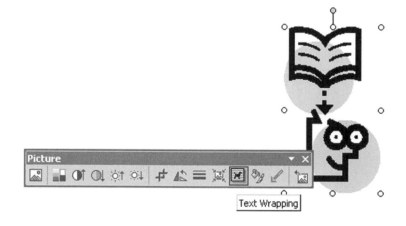

Insert a saved image: Click the toolbar button 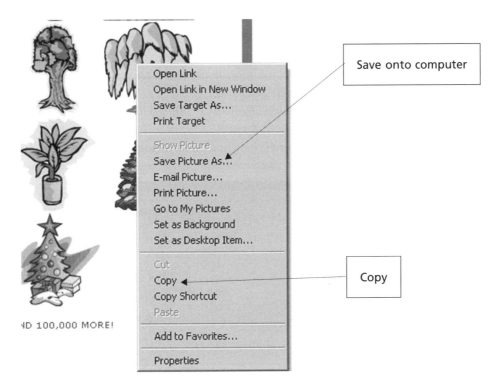 or select **Insert – Picture – from File** and locate the file within your computer. Preview it in the window and click the Insert button to add it to the page. (See the earlier section on importing files and objects.)

Copy a picture across: having drawn or scanned in a picture, or opened a camera image, make sure it is selected and then right-click to find the Copy option or select this from the **Edit** menu. Click in place in your document and click **Paste.**

With a Web image, right-click to open the menu. (As you cannot use original artwork that is subject to copyright, search using the word 'clipart' to help locate free images.) You can select *Save Picture As* if you want it to remain on your computer for future use, but select *Copy* to copy it straight away. Once again, return to your document and paste it in.

One problem you may find with Web images is that sometimes the picture was created as a hyperlink, opening a new Web page when clicked. As this can be a nuisance when editing a picture, right-click and remove the link.

Borders

You can border selected text and/or shade the background with a colour by selecting options from the **Format – Borders and Shading** menu. You will need to click a Setting: option e.g. Box or Shadow to add the full border, or use the Preview buttons to set odd borders e.g. without a top or side line.

Check the entry in the Apply to: box if you want the border to extend across the paragraph or simply emphasise the actual text. You can also add attractive borders to

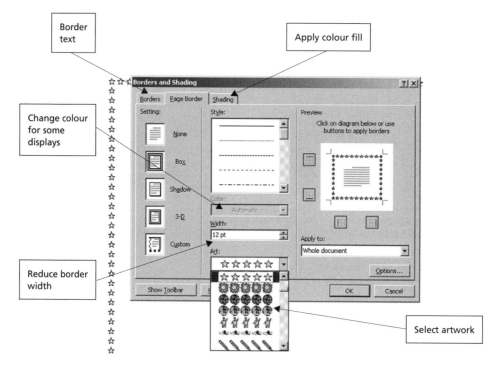

a whole page by clicking the Page Border tab and selecting a picture from the Art: box. Change the point size of any artwork if it makes the border too wide and apply colours to black and white designs.

Columns

Setting text in columns can sometimes make the words easier to read. Either start with the format on or apply columns to a selected block of text.

1. Click the Columns toolbar button ▦ and drag across to apply a two or three column format. You will notice that shading on the ruler shows you have set columns and, when you reach the bottom of the page you will continue into the second column automatically.
2. To add a line between the columns, or set different column widths, go to **Format – Columns** to open the dialogue box.

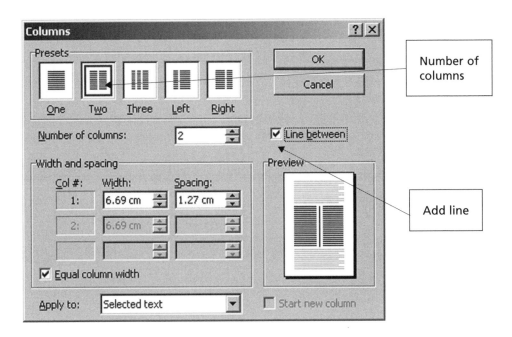

3. Having created columns, you may want to return to normal typing at the end of the text. Do this by pressing *Enter*, opening the Columns dialogue box and selecting One column. In the Apply to: box, make sure you pick *This point forward*.
4. Within the columns, if you would like the second or third column to start with a particular word or sentence or need to readjust the text to balance the two

columns more equally, click in front of the word you want at the top of the second column and then open the **Insert** menu and select **Break – Column break.**

Bullet formats

Lists can look more fun if items are separated by coloured or shaped bullets rather than the plainer ones automatically selected. To change them, select the full list and go to **Format – Bullets and Numbering.** You may see a style you like in the boxes on display, but find more examples by clicking the Customize button. Here you can select Character to open the Symbol box or Picture to display coloured bullets. If you have a picture on your computer, you can even use this as bullets if you click *Import* and locate the picture file.

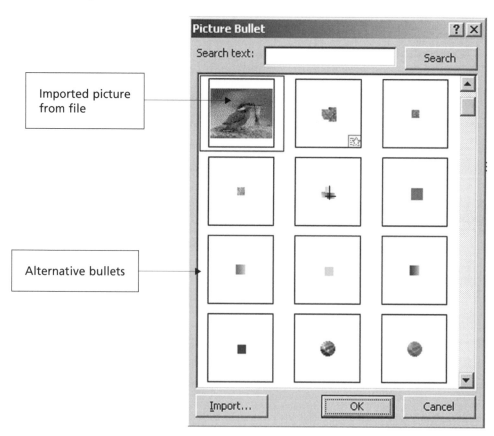

Imported picture from file

Alternative bullets

WordArt

As an alternative to normal text, add words in the form of a shaped object known as *WordArt*. You can add and amend this in 4 simple steps:

1. Click the toolbar button on the *Drawing* toolbar to open the gallery and select a style from the display before clicking *OK*.

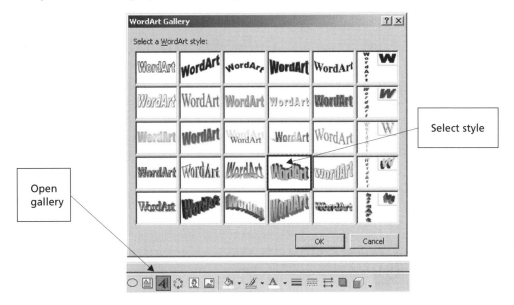

2. Type your own text in the box, making changes to the font if you want to at this stage. Then click *OK* to return to your document.

3. The *WordArt* will appear and if you click it you will show the toolbar. Use this to amend colours, shapes, spacing etc. As with pictures from the *Clip Art* gallery, apply a text wrap to allow you to drag the *WordArt* around the page.

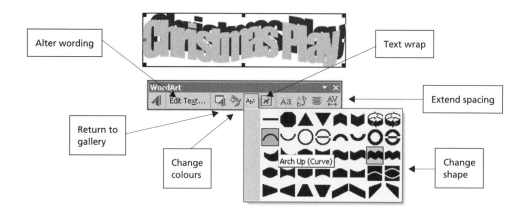

MACROS

When you regularly carry out the same repetitive tasks, whether complex or those as simple as changing the page orientation and adding your name and contact number to a footer, *Word* allows you to save these actions in the form of a program called a *macro*. Once created, you can run the macro any time to carry out the job for you.

1. When you are ready to carry out your task, open the **Tools** menu and select **Macro – Record New Macro.**
2. In the dialog box, type a name to identify the macro – do not leave any spaces between words – and add a short description e.g. *my name Arial 12 in footer*. You could click the buttons to add the macro to your toolbar at this stage, or create a shortcut via the keyboard if you will use the macro regularly.

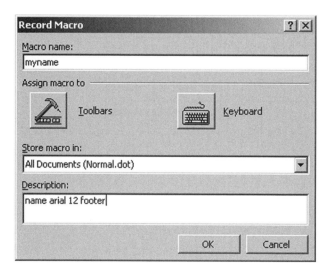

3. Click *OK* and a button will appear on your screen. Now carry out your task as efficiently as possible. Every key stroke and mouse click will be 'recorded' to create the program. Note that you won't be able to select words by dragging the mouse – hold Shift and click an arrow/cursor key in the appropriate direction instead.

4. When you have finished, click the *Stop* button.

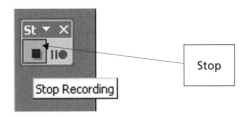

5. Next time you need to perform the same task, open the **Tools** menu and select **Macros**. Select the correct macro in the window and click *Run*. It will now carry out your tedious task for you. The window also offers the option to delete an unwanted macro or edit it if you need to make minor changes.

6. To add the macro as a button to your toolbar so that you can click it to perform your task without using the menus, click the *Add* or *Remove* Buttons arrow at the end of any toolbar. Click *Customize* and find the Macros category from the list. Click the labelled macro button and drag it up onto your toolbar.

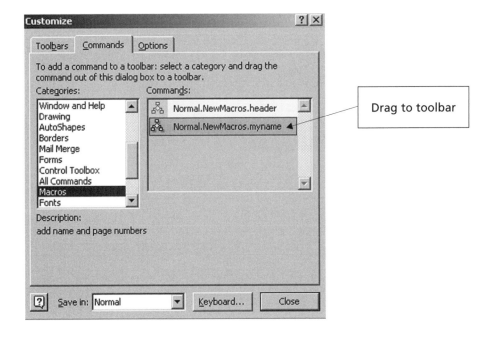

SYMBOLS AND SPECIAL CHARACTERS

When adding a French or German name to correspondence, it is pleasing for your respondent to see their name printed out accurately with the appropriate accent. In the same way, adding little pictures of scissors or books, a tick in a box or the copyright symbol © may all be necessary at some time.

Using a version of *Office* earlier than *Word 2002*, you need to add accents in the following way:

1. Hold Ctrl and press the relevant punctuation symbol e.g. use a colon for an umlaut and an apostrophe for accent acute. If the symbol is at the *top* of a key, hold Shift at the same time.
2. Press the appropriate letter key e.g. e or u as normal
3. Type the next letter and the e or u will now appear as é or ü.

For symbols (and accents for *Office XP*), find them from the **Insert – Symbol** menu option. There is a wide choice of fonts each offering a different range of symbols, as well as a separate tab for characters such as copyright or Trademark. Recently used symbols may be available on a shortcut bar.

Having located and selected your symbol, click *Insert* and then close the window to return to your document.

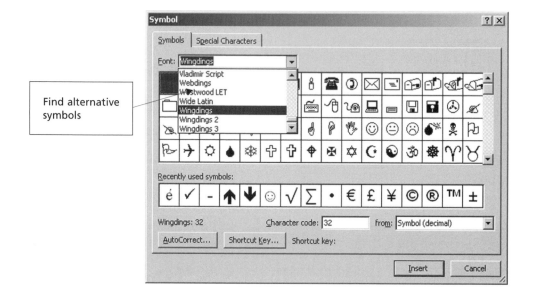

Find alternative symbols

DETECTING OTHER PEOPLE'S SETTINGS

When asked to edit someone else's document, you may be faced with a strange layout that doesn't seem to make sense. By looking very carefully at all the instructions the computer has been given, you may be able to locate an unwanted key stroke or changed setting which you can then put right.

Key strokes

If you cannot apply a paragraph format or print a document properly, you may need to know if someone has used a tab key, space bar or pressed Enter. To do this, you must turn on the Show/Hide [¶] button which reveals all the key strokes in the form of special symbols e.g. an arrow for tab and dots for spaces.

I·have·used·a·tab·key· →   ·space·bar·several·times·····and·then·pressed·Enter¶
¶

Once these are revealed, corrective action is often simple. For example, if the Enter key has been pressed at the end of every line *within* a paragraph, each line will be treated as a new paragraph when you try to apply an alignment. Simply delete these unwanted key strokes and close up the spaces to return to normal.

Menu options

When a paragraph simply won't start at the left margin, or you cannot carry on with your normal line spacing, you need to find out if an unusual setting has been imposed by mistake. Extra tabs or changed markers on the ruler may reveal the problem but it is easier to open the most likely menu e.g. **Format – Paragraph** and check all the settings boxes. If you spot the culprit e.g. a hanging indent or extra spaces inserted after each paragraph, you will be able to take these off again.

Hanging indent set

Once these are revea[...]
Enter key has [...]
each line will b[...]
alignment. Sim[...]
spaces to retur[...]

When a paragraph sir[...]
all the wrong spacing[...]
imposed by mistake.

Extra spacing
added after
paragraph

Return to
0 pt

Select
(none)

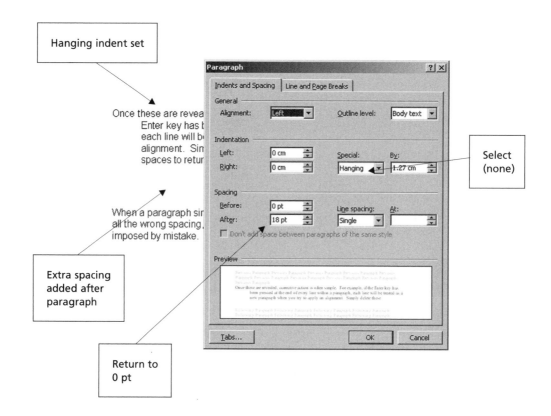

Spreadsheets and Charts

If you haven't ever used a spreadsheet package before, imagine a large pad of graph paper. Each sheet is like a huge page of paper covered in thousands of squares. The squares – known as cells – are arranged in columns labelled A, B, C, etc. and rows numbered 1, 2, 3, etc. Any cell you click becomes the 'active' cell – it will display a black border and anything you type appears inside and can be formatted in the normal way. The cell's contents are also displayed, and can be edited, in the Formula bar.

Cells are referred to by their column letter and row number e.g. D7 below.

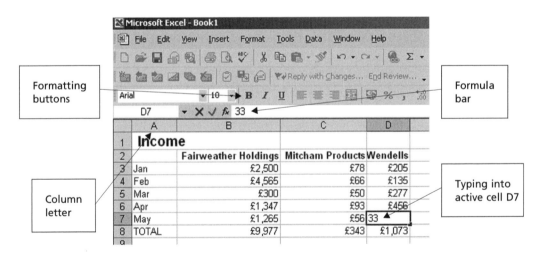

It is quite likely that you will be asked to work on excessively large spreadsheets, covering thousands of columns and rows and which may extend across a number of sheets or even separate files (Workbooks). Although they may appear daunting, follow the guidance in this chapter to master all the 'tricky' tasks you may need to carry out.

In particular, you may need to:

◆ Understand underlying mathematical principles
◆ Protect cells
◆ Use a variety of functions
◆ Name cells or use an absolute cell reference
◆ Apply different formats
◆ Work across multiple worksheets or files
◆ Find information
◆ Analyse data using a pivot table

Depending on your role, you may also need to produce charts and graphs as an alternative method for presenting numerical information, either to print out or to copy into a word processed document or include in a *PowerPoint* presentation. To help you, this chapter ends with advice on producing and customising charts.

A FEW WORDS ABOUT USING NUMBERS

Although *Excel* takes the pain out of calculations, it is important to understand some of the mathematical principles underlying the program, as you must always type your instructions – the formulae – accurately. You should also be able to estimate the likely results of any calculations so that you can pick up mistakes quickly.

BODMAS

At some time you may need to create quite complex formulae and write them in a way that ensures the calculations are performed accurately. You therefore need to know that *Excel* carries out calculations in a particular order, following the BOD-MAS (or BIDMAS) rule:

1st **B**rackets
$(3+4)/2 = 7/2 = 3.5$
not: $3 + 4/2 = 3 + 2 = 5$

2nd **O**rder/**I**ndex (or Power)
$3 + 2^3 = 3 + 8 = 11$
not: $5^3 = 125$

3rd   **D**ivision and **M**ultiplication (priority from left to right)
             15 – 2 x 6 = 15 – 12 = 3
             not: 13 x 6 = 78

4th   **A**ddition and **S**ubtraction (priority from left to right)
             2 + 7 x 4 + 2/2 – 3 = 2 + 28 + 1 – 3 = 31 – 3 = 28
             not: 9 x 6/2 – 3 = 27 – 3 = 24

Remember that you should always start a formula by typing = and try to use the address of a cell e.g. B12 or C4 in your formulae, rather than the raw figures so that you are instructing *Excel* to base calculations on the *contents* of a cell at any time. This will mean that changing any figures on a spreadsheet will update the calculations automatically.

Excel uses these operators:

+ add

- subtract

* multiply

/ divide

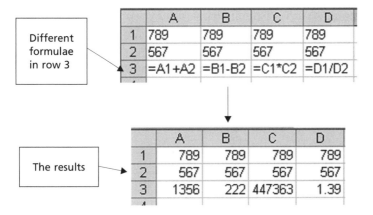

Percentage

Percentage means parts of a hundred.

100% is 100/100 which cancels down to 1 – the whole

50% is 50/100 which cancels down to ½

25% is 25/100 which cancels down to ¼

75% is 75/100 which cancels down to ¾

20% is 20/100 which cancels down to $^1/5$

1. To work out the percentage (e.g. 2% or 30%) of a number (e.g. 65), multiply them together:

2% of 65 = 2% x 65 = 2/100 x 65 = 130/100 = 13/10 = 1.3

30% of 65 = 30% x 65 = 30/100 x 65 = 3/10 x 65 = 195/10 = 19.5

You should now be able to carry out a common task which is to work out the final cost of an item that is being discounted. To do this, you need to use a formula that will subtract the discount e.g. 8% of the original price (£237.50 in the following example) from this figure.

Remembering BODMAS, you can use brackets so that the formula will look like this:

Final price = original price – (discount x original price)

$\qquad$ = £237.50 – (8% x £237.50)

$\qquad$ = B2-(C2*B2)

D2	▼		f_x =B2-(C2*B2)	
	A	B	C	D
1	Item	Price	Discount	Final Price
2	Encyclopaedia	£237.50	8%	£218.50
3				

2. To convert a fraction such as 3/5 into a percentage, remember that a fraction is part of a whole and 100/100 (100%) is also a whole.

So the true problem is: 3 out of 5 is the same as **what** out of 100?

$$\frac{3}{5} = \frac{?}{100}$$

$$\frac{3 \times 100}{5} = ? = \frac{300}{5} = 60$$

So the answer is 60%

Note: In *Excel,* be careful when formatting cells. Applying a percentage format multiplies a fraction or decimal by 100 e.g. if you type 0.25 in a cell and format to percentage the cell will display 25%. To *type* 25% in a cell, *don't* format the cell to percentages and then enter 25 or you will end up with 2500%. Instead, type the % symbol manually. The figure will still be recognised by *Excel* as 25%.

PROTECTING CELLS

You may not be aware of this when working with spreadsheets in the normal way, but cells in a spreadsheet are automatically locked. If you *protect* the worksheet, no-one will be able to amend any entries. You can use this facility if you create sensitive spreadsheets where another member of staff needs to be able to make some changes. To allow *specific* cells only to be edited, unlock them first before protecting the rest of the sheet.

Carry this out by following these steps:

1. Select the cells that you want open to editing and go to **Format – Cells – Protection**. Make sure you take off the tick in the Locked checkbox before clicking *OK.*

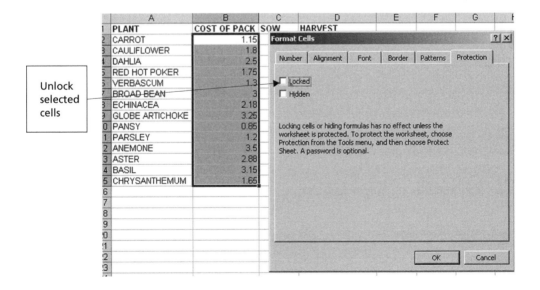

2. Open the **Tools** menu and select **Protection – Protect Sheet.** In the dialog box that opens, select the option to allow changes to unlocked cells and, if required, add a password to restrict access.

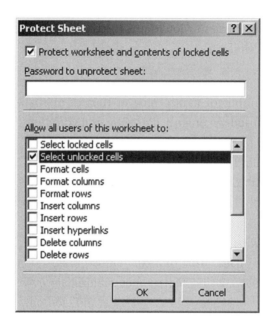

3. When you return to the sheet, you will find that you can now only click in the unlocked cells.

FUNCTIONS

You may already have met some basic functions that speed up totalling and averaging columns of numbers, but there are many others that can be useful.

To enter a function, you need to use the actual term recognised by *Excel* e.g. SUM, AVERAGE etc. and include the range of cells to which the function will apply. To add cell addresses to a formula quickly, click and drag across the range and they will be entered as the address of the first, a colon and then the address of the last. You will, however, still need to type the brackets e.g. (C2:C8).

In the following examples, you would click in B16 and type the appropriate function:

	A	B
1	PLANT	COST OF PACK
2	CARROT	1.15
3	CAULIFLOWER	1.8
4	DAHLIA	2.5
5	RED HOT POKER	1.75
6	VERBASCUM	1.3
7	BROAD BEAN	3
8	ECHINACEA	2.18
9	GLOBE ARTICHOKE	3.25
10	PANSY	0.85
11	PARSLEY	1.2
12	ANEMONE	3.5
13	ASTER	2.88
14	BASIL	3.15
15	CHRYSANTHEMUM	1.65
16		

For machines with *Office XP* installed, you will also be offered these functions if you click the arrow next to the AutoSum button. However, in earlier versions of *Excel* the button only provides the SUM totalling function.

1. To total the cost of all seed packs, use the SUM function:
   =SUM (B2:B15). Alternatively, select the range of cells and click the AutoSum button to add a total to the next empty cell.

2. To find the average cost of seed packs, use the AVERAGE function:
   =AVERAGE (B2:B15). This will total the prices and then divide by the number of packs. (As an alternative, you could find the total in B16 and then work out the average on the next row by dividing the total by the number of packs using the formula =B16/14.)

3. To count up the number of packs of seeds, use the COUNT function:
   =COUNT (B2:B15). To count cells that contain a text entry, you must use the function **COUNTA**.

4. To find the most expensive pack, use the MAXIMUM function:
   = MAX (B2:B15)

5. To find the cheapest pack, use the MINIMUM function:
   =MIN (B2:B15)

If you look at the bottom of your screen, you will see the total of any selected cells showing on the status bar. A quick way to find the average, maximum etc. for your cells if you just want to know the answer rather than enter it on the spreadsheet is to right-click the figure and select an alternative function from the list.

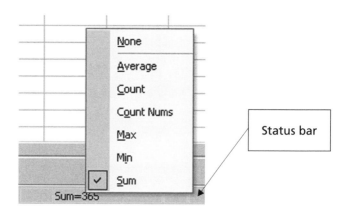

IF function

This function is different as it compares each entry row by row. It is based on the following logic:

If statement A is true, display X, if not display Y

In *Excel* this is written as follows:

=IF(statement,"text if true","text if false")

For the seed packs, you might want to know which seeds cost more than £2. If they cost more, display the word *yes,* but if they cost less display the word *no.*

The statement is: *the cost of a pack is more than £2.*

1. Click in C2 and enter **=IF(**
2. You want to know if Carrot seeds cost more than £2, so this is written **B2>2**
3. Add a comma and then the text you want to see if it is true i.e. *yes*. Text should be in quotation marks so this is written "yes" (although you do not include quotes if you wanted to display a number instead of text entry).
4. Finally, add a comma and type the text you will see if the answer is not true i.e. "no".

The full function is written **=IF(B2>2,"yes","no")**

	A	B	C
1	PLANT	COST OF PACK	MORE THAN £2
2	CARROT	1.15	=IF(B2>2,"yes","no")
3	CAULIFLOWER	1.8	
4	DAHLIA	2.5	
5	RED HOT POKER	1.75	
6	VERBASCUM	1.3	
7	BROAD BEAN	3	
8	ECHINACEA	2.18	
9	GLOBE ARTICHOKE	3.25	
10	PANSY	0.85	
11	PARSLEY	1.2	
12	ANEMONE	3.5	
13	ASTER	2.88	
14	BASIL	3.15	
15	CHRYSANTHEMUM	1.65	

This function can be replicated down the column, as the next cell will contain a reference to Cauliflower seeds and the formula will be written =IF(B3>2,"yes","no"). The rest of the seed packs will be compared in the same way.

C5		f_x =IF(B5>2,"yes","no")	
	A	B	C
1	PLANT	COST OF PACK	MORE THAN £2
2	CARROT	1.15	no
3	CAULIFLOWER	1.8	no
4	DAHLIA	2.5	yes
5	RED HOT POKER	1.75	no
6	VERBASCUM	1.3	no
7	BROAD BEAN	3	yes
8	ECHINACEA	2.18	yes
9	GLOBE ARTICHOKE	3.25	yes
10	PANSY	0.85	no
11	PARSLEY	1.2	no
12	ANEMONE	3.5	yes
13	ASTER	2.88	yes
14	BASIL	3.15	yes
15	CHRYSANTHEMUM	1.65	no

To help with any function, you can always click the insert Function button marked *fx* on the Formula Bar, select the relevant function and complete the boxes that are offered.

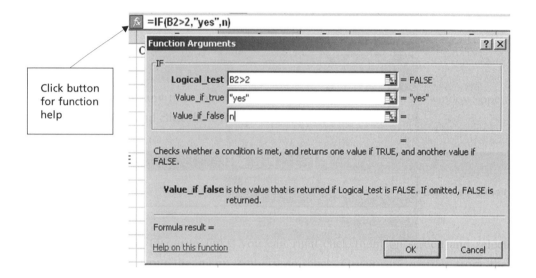

Click button for function help

IMPORTING DATA

In many organisations, data will have been prepared in a grid or table using a different application e.g. *Works* or even *Word*, and you may want to add it to a new or existing spreadsheet. Fortunately, *Excel* is very accommodating. All you need to do is select all the data in the original file and click the *Copy* option. With your spreadsheet open, click *one* cell e.g. A1 or further down an existing sheet, and then right-click and select *Paste*. The data should appear and you can continue working as normal.

To copy across a database from *Access*, you may prefer to use the *Office Links* facility described in the chapter on databases. However, as the data in a database table is set out in a similar way to a spreadsheet, you can also simply copy and paste it across.

Copying within *Excel*
If you are copying from another worksheet or even on the same sheet and want to copy cells whose contents were created using formulae, there will be a problem with straightforward pasting as the cell addresses will no longer apply. Instead, use the

Edit menu to select **Paste Special**. You can now choose whether to paste only the values or to include the formulae.

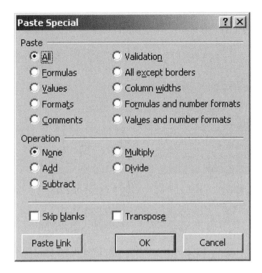

INSERTING NEW COLUMNS OR ROWS

At any time, you may want to add extra rows or columns of data into a spreadsheet or delete redundant information without leaving blank cells.

◆ Click the column letter header to the *right* of a new column, or row header box *below* the position for a new row. With the row or column selected, go to **Insert – Columns** (or **Rows**). The new column or row will slide into place and header letters or numbers will be adjusted automatically.

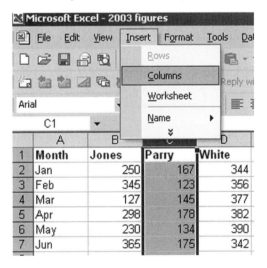

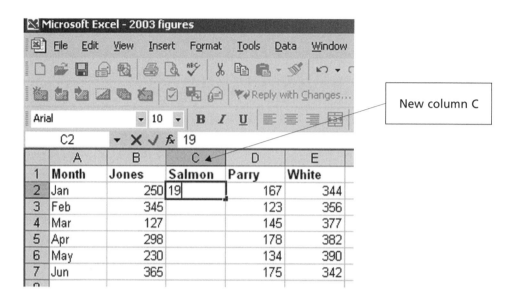

- To add more than one extra column or row, select that number of header cells first.
- To delete one or more columns or rows, click the header letters or numbers to select the entire column or row and then go to **Edit – Delete.** Using the Delete key on your keyboard will only delete cell entries and leave empty cells in place.

ABSOLUTE CELLS

Copying formulae across rows or down columns is very simple: drag the 'fill handle' in the bottom, right-hand corner of the cell when the pointer shows a small black cross. As formulae normally contain 'relative' cell addresses, these will adjust e.g. reference to B2 will become B3, B4, B5 etc. as you move down the column.

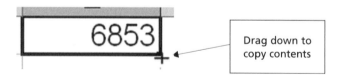

Very often, you will want to refer to the contents of one particular cell when carrying out a calculation that will be copied/replicated across a spreadsheet e.g. if applying a discount or percentage to a range of entries, or converting units of measure. If you try to copy the formula down a column in the normal way, the contents of this particular cell will *also* be copied down which will result in errors.

	A	B	C
1	Item	Cost	Discount
2	Walnut	25	=B2*A10
3	Mahogany	18	=B3*A11
4	Beech	30	=B4*A12
5	Oak	27	=B5*A13
6	Cherry	43	=B6*A14
7			
8			
9	Discount		
10	0.05		

All should include reference to A10

To fix the cell address in a formula that is going to be copied, you have two options: naming the cell or using the absolute cell reference.

Naming cells

Any cell, or range of cells, can be given a name. You can then refer to them by that name and only the named cell will be included in your calculations. To name a cell or range, select it and then go to **Insert – Name – Define**. Type the name for the cell in the box or accept the name that appears and click *OK*.

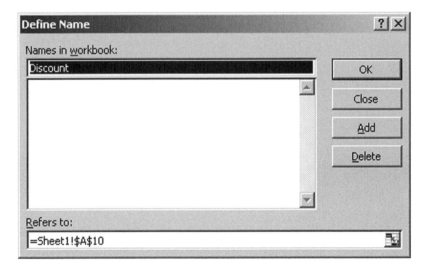

Using the name in your formula rather than cell address means you can copy it down the column accurately.

| C3 | ▼ | | fx | =B3*Discount |

	A	B	C	D
1	Item	Cost	Discount	Final Price
2	Walnut	£25	£1.25	
3	Mahogany	£18	£0.90	
4	Beech	£30	£1.50	
5	Oak	£27	£1.35	
6	Cherry	£43	£2.15	
7				
8				
9	Discount			
10	5%			
11				

Absolute cell reference

If you prefix a cell address with dollar symbols $, *Excel* recognises this as the absolute address and it will not change as you copy a formula down the column.

1. Enter the first formula as normal and then add dollar signs to the cell address you wish to fix. You can type the $$ manually or use the following shortcut.
2. In the Formula Bar, click between column letter (e.g. A) and row number (e.g. 10) for the cell and press the function key F4. Dollar symbols will appear. If you keep clicking F4, you can partially fix the address (e.g. A$10, so that when copied it will become B$10, C$10 etc.) or take them off completely.

| ▼ | ✗ ✓ | fx | =B2*$A$10 |

B	C	D	
Cost	Discount	Final Price	
£25	=B2*$A$10		
£18			
£30			
£27			
£43			

3. Click the tick or press Enter and then copy this formula down the column. All cells will now contain a reference to A10.

	A	B	C
1	Item	Cost	Discount
2	Walnut	25	=B2*$A$10
3	Mahogany	18	=B3*$A$10
4	Beech	30	=B4*$A$10
5	Oak	27	=B5*$A$10
6	Cherry	43	=B6*$A$10
7			
8			
9	Discount		
10	0.05		

FORMATS

When it comes to formatting, spreadsheets are very logical. Click any cell or select a range of cells and then use normal word processing buttons on the toolbar to change entries to bold, italic, centre alignment etc. or open the **Format – Cells** menu and select options from the **Font, Number** or **Alignment** tabs.

Error messages

Whenever *Excel* carries out a calculation, it puts the answer in the cell using a general format. As this may have a number of decimal places, the column may not be wide enough for the full display. You will see #### appearing instead of the figure. Simply widen the column to view the figures.

Customised dates

To make your dates or numbers look right, you need to format them via the **Format – Cells – Number** menu. However, you may not see exactly the style you want even after scrolling down through the list of styles on offer. Fortunately, you can create your very own style and impose it on the machine.

If we take dates as an example, perhaps you would like to see the format **22 Jan 04** but all you can find is 22 January 2004.

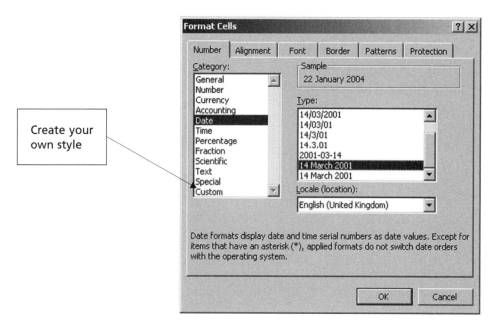

Create your own style

If you click the word *Custom* in the Category list, you will be offered a further range of dates. These are expressed in terms of d (for day), m (for month) and y (for year). The number of letters is translated into the characters in the display, with mmmm displaying the full name of the month.

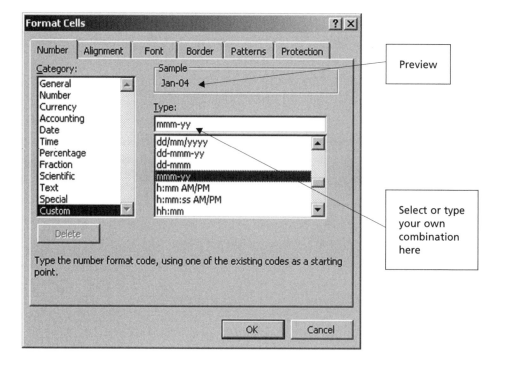

Preview

Select or type your own combination here

dd/mm/yy will display 22/01/04

dd/mm/yyyy will display 22/01/2004

dd/mmm/yy will display 22-Jan-04

dd/mmmm/yy will display 22 January 04

If you don't see the exact style you want, type into the box until the Sample displays your choice and then click *OK*.

Column headings

You may want to retain narrow widths for your columns but still display a long entry. Do this by selecting the cell, opening the **Format – Cells – Alignment** menu and clicking on *Wrap text*.

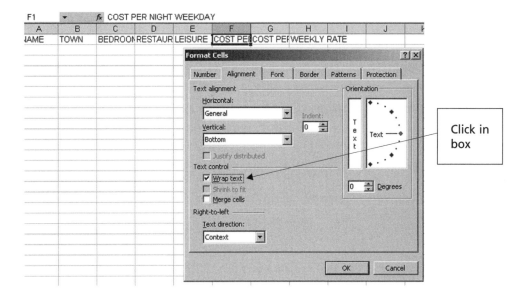

You may need to increase the row height or drag the border to prevent words being split but you will now be able to see the entire entry and still keep the column narrow. Once you have one deeper cell, you can set entries in neighbouring cells centrally or at the top or bottom of the cell using the vertical alignment options.

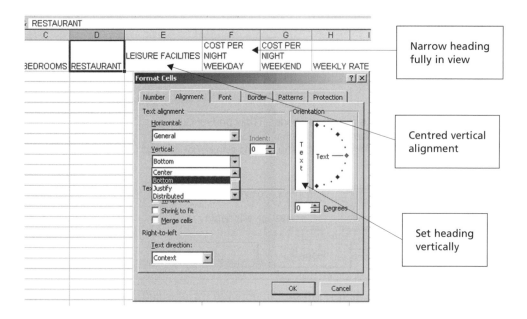

You can also display a heading vertically if you select the range of cells and select the vertical Text orientation box, drag the red pointer or set the measure to + or – 90 Degrees. Click the *Merge cells* button and then *OK*.

PRINTING

Depending on the default settings, your spreadsheet may or may not print out showing gridlines. To select your preferred display, open the **File – Page Setup** menu and click the Gridline checkbox on the *Sheet* tab. On the *Margin* tab, you can also choose to set the spreadsheet data in the middle of a page by clicking the *Centring* options.

Normally, only that portion of the spreadsheet with entries will print, but if you want to print selected columns only, select them with the mouse and then click *Selection* in the *Print* what box.

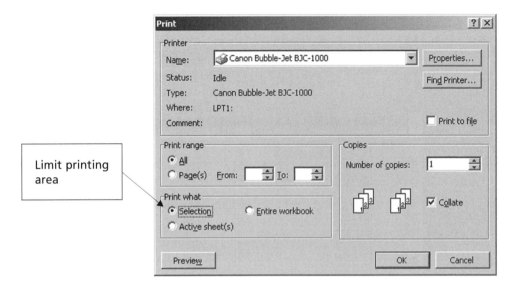

GIVE IT A TICK

It may seem a silly little thing, but people often use spreadsheets for questionnaires and surveys and want to be able to add a tick ✓ to a cell. Unfortunately, the option that has always been available in *Word* (**Insert – Symbol**) is not available in *Excel 2000*, although it has now been added to *Excel XP (2002)*.

If you have the older version of the software, here are a couple of ways to add this symbol:

◆ Open a *Word* document, find the tick from the **Insert – Symbol** menu e.g. under Wingdings fonts, click to select it and then press the Insert button and close the symbol box. Now *copy* and *paste* the tick that will have been added to the page into an *Excel* cell.

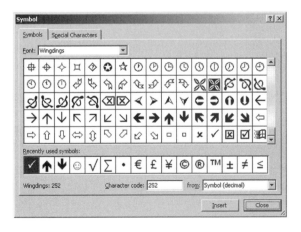

◆ You can now use copy and paste within *Excel* to add the symbol to further cells in your spreadsheet. (The cell being copied will show flashing dots – a marquee – round it to show which cell is being copied, so remove these by pressing the *Escape* key when you have finished copying.)

◆ You may have the component *Character Map* installed on your machine (usually under **Programs – Accessories – System Tools**) which works in a similar way. Open the window and find the symbol, click it and then click *Copy*. Now paste it into a cell but make sure you format the cell to the *same* font e.g. Wingdings or you will display a different symbol or character (e.g. the letter P or a square).

CREATE A SERIES

One shortcut worth using is when you want row or column labels to display dates, months or days of the week. If you type one entry e.g. *Monday* and then copy this down using the fill handle in the bottom, right-hand corner of the cell, the next cells will display Tuesday, Wednesday, Thursday etc. as *Excel* recognises the date series.

To cancel this effect, type the same date twice, select *both* cells and copy down from the second. However, if you type two *numbers* into adjacent cells and copy down from the second you can create an incremental series.

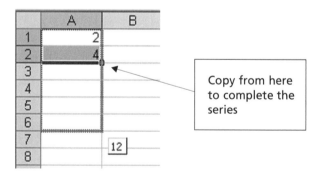

Copy from here to complete the series

WORKING WITH WORKSHEETS

Freeze panes

Large spreadsheets often have column or row headings that need to be viewed when entering data. However, once you have scrolled down the rows a short way, you won't be able to view the headings in row 1.

To fix the position of headings, so that your columns and rows roll behind them, freeze them as follows:

1. Click the first cell to the right of any column you want to freeze e.g. B1, or below a header row e.g. A2 and then select **Window – Freeze Panes**. To be able to view both column and row headings, click B2.

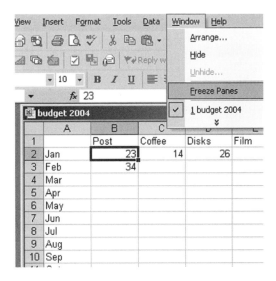

2. Lines will appear down the boundary of column A and below row 1 to show where they are frozen.
3. Scroll to the right to enter figures in column H or I and you will see that columns B – D have disappeared behind column A. You will now always be able to view e.g. the months when entering your figures. The column headings will also remain in place if you scroll down below row 15 or 16.

B – D behind A

4. Take off the freeze at any time by selecting **Window – Unfreeze Panes**.

Naming sheets

You don't need to retain the names of sheets as Sheet1, Sheet2 etc. Double click the tab at the bottom of the screen and rename them. You can also insert or move sheets. Add new sheets from the **Insert** menu, and drag them to new positions if you want them re-ordered. To select a number of sheets, click the first and then hold Shift as you click the last.

Formulae across sheets and files

Within one workbook, you are likely to have data on a number of sheets that sometimes needs to be referred to in calculations e.g. monthly figures used to create an overall total for the quarter. Simply click the correct sheet tab and then the cells when creating your formulae and the addresses will be added as normal.

When drawing information from different sheets, each sheet will be referred to by name plus an exclamation mark. For example, if adding the contents of A6 from three sheets, the formula will look like this:

B2	▼		f_x	=Sheet1!A6+Sheet2!A6+Sheet3!A6		
	A	B	C	D	E	
2	Quarterly total	431				

If you had renamed the sheets it might appear as:

=January!A6+February!A6+March!A6

To use data from different *Workbook* files, you need to open them and then click the cells as above. Here, any external workbook will be referred to by name plus the file extension *.xls* and the whole will be placed in square brackets. You will also note that the actual cells will contain an absolute cell reference and complex file names will have quote marks round them.

e.g. ='[budget 2004.xls]Sheet1'!$A$10+'[budget 2003.xls]Sheet1'!$A$10

Although you can type the formula including punctuation yourself, clicking a cell on each sheet when creating your formulae will automatically enter the appropriate identification and will ensure you do not make any mistakes.

Arranging Windows

You can move between open *Workbooks* quickly by holding Ctrl and pressing the tab key, and between sheets by using Ctrl and Page Up or Page Down. However, when working with data from more than one *Workbook*, it is much easier if you can see all the cells at the same time. Open the **Window** menu, click **Arrange** and then choose an arrangement such as *Vertical*. Drag out any boundaries if relevant data is hidden. The active *Workbook* will have a blue title bar and you must click any *Workbook* to activate it before you can copy the data into your formula.

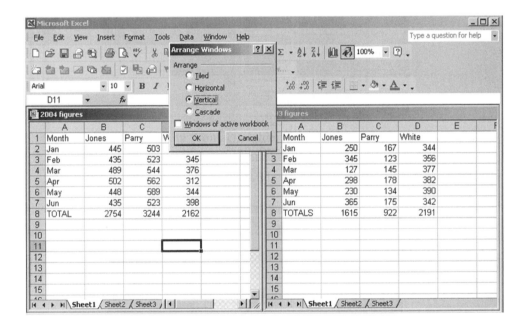

FINDING INFORMATION

Many organisations set up databases in *Excel*. If there is no requirement to relate different sets of data, a relational database such as *Access* may not have been used and you will therefore have to work with the spreadsheet application. Fortunately, it is perfectly adequate for straightforward storing and searching of data.

Here are four basic functions that can make life easy when using *Excel* as a database application:

Re-ordering entries

When looking for a particular name or date in a jumble of entries, it can help if you sort the block of data and re-order the records e.g. by name, price or date etc. Do this by selecting *all* the data including column headings and then opening the **Data – Sort** menu. (Without column headings selected, each column will be labelled 1, 2, 3 etc in the Sort box and so will be less easy to work with.)

Choose the first order of sort, and perhaps a second or third if several items have the same first entry, and check that each one is in ascending (alphabetical) or descending order. Click *OK* and the records will now be re-ordered.

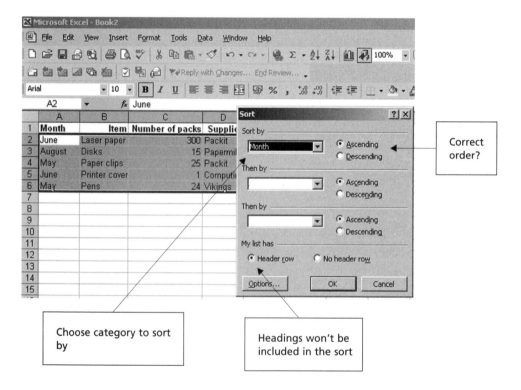

Updating entries

A common task is to keep the database up to date, so that it contains the latest names and address details. For a database with thousands of records, finding the correct entry manually could take some time, so you need to use the **Edit – Replace** facility.

Having completed the *Find what:* and *Replace with:* boxes, if you know there is only one entry to change, or that all the entries should be changed, you can click *Replace All*. However, if you wanted to change Paul Drefuss's name to Paulo, but not Paul Duchamps', for example, you would need to keep clicking *Find Next* and check by eye. When the correct entry is selected, change it by clicking *Replace*.

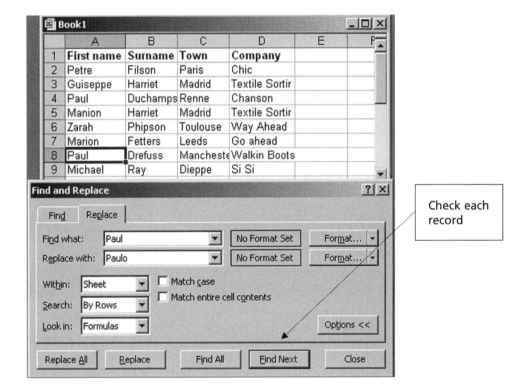

Check each record

Using a form

Many people prefer to enter information into a database by using a form. This lets you view a complete record, rather than a table of all the records together.

Create a form by selecting all the records and going to **Data – Form**. When the form appears, click *New* to add new records.

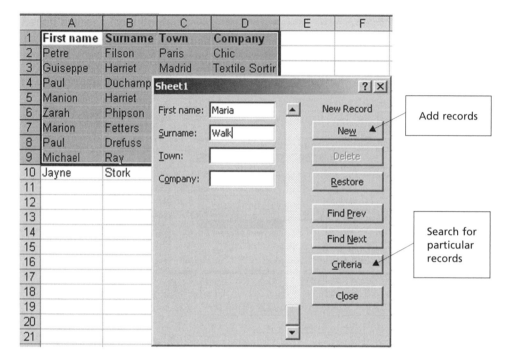

Searching

To search for a particular record or set of records, you can use the form. Click *Criteria* and you will see empty boxes. Enter your search criteria in the correct boxes e.g. Manchester in the Town box will find any records of suppliers from this town. Click the *Find Next* and *Previous* buttons to move through the records.

To view more than one record at a time when searching, you need to apply a filter. Go to **Data – Filter – AutoFilter** and down-facing arrows will appear next to each column heading (known as a Field name). If you click an arrow, you will see all the entries made in that field. Click any entry to find matching records.

	A	B	C	D
1	First nam ▾	Surnan ▾	Town ▾	Company ▾
2	Petre	Filson	(All)	Chic
3	Guiseppe	Harriet	(Top 10...)	Textile Sortir
4	Paul	Ducha	(Custom...)	Chanson
5	Manion	Harriet	Dieppe	Textile Sortir
6	Zarah	Phipso	Glasgow	Way Ahead
7	Marion	Fetters	Leeds	Go ahead
8	Paul	Drefus	Madrid	Walkin Boots
9	Michael	Ray	Manchester	Si Si
10	Jayne	Stork	Paris	Fabric Fashions
11	Maria	Walker	Renne	Cozee
			Toulouse	
			Glasgow	
			Madrid	

For a more complex search, click the *Custom . . .* entry for any field and you will open the dialog box. Here you can select a logical statement e.g. greater than, contains, ends with etc. and type your own entry or select from the available list. You can also repeat searches to filter out more and more records.

For example, you could find which suppliers have first names beginning with M, and then search for any Madrid suppliers amongst them:

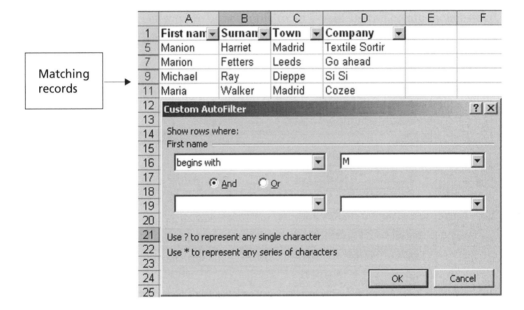

You can print the selected records if required and then take off the filter by selecting (All) from the list, or use the menu and click **Data – Filter – Show All**.

PIVOT TABLES

More complex analysis of data is possible if you create a Pivot Table. This allows you to organise your columns and rows quite differently from the original layout and calculate totals, averages or maximum figures etc.

Design the table

Use the Wizard and click *Next* each time to work through the steps.

1. Select the data and go to **Data – Pivot Table**. Check that the correct data source is to be analysed.

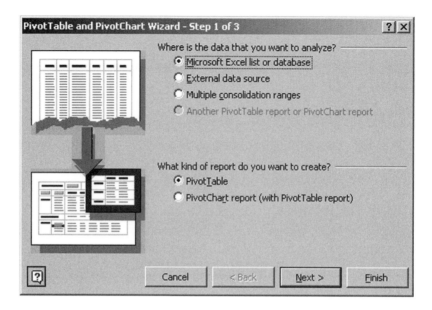

2. If you didn't select the cells first, click the red button and highlight the records you want to analyse. Click the button again to return to the Wizard.

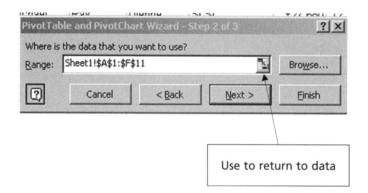

Use to return to data

3. Decide whether to place the table on a new sheet or not and then click *Finish*. To place the table on the same sheet as your data, clicking the cell where you want the table to start adds the cell address to the box provided.
4. You can now create an appropriate design for your Pivot Table. On the left, you will be offered all the headings (field names) in your database, and you can drag any field across to a chosen position in the table.

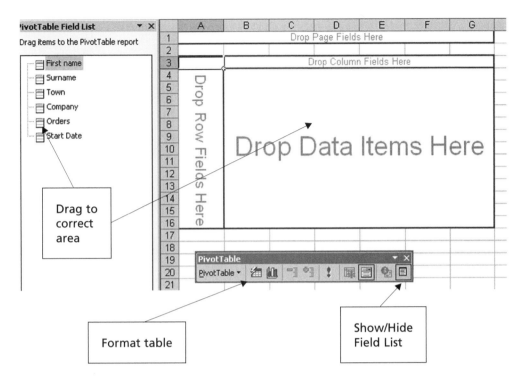

Analyse the data

There are four areas to which you can drag fields from your database: the Row fields, Data items, Page fields and Column fields. Simply drag fields on and off these areas to experiment with changing the presentation of your data.

To find out how much each company's total orders come to, for example, you could drag Company to the **Row Fields** area and Orders to the **Data Items** area. The result is shown below:

	A	B
1	Drop Page Fields Here	
2		
3	Sum of Orders	
4	Company ▼	Total
5	Chanson	13500
6	Chic	23000
7	Cozee	17950
8	Fabric Fashions	32550
9	Go ahead	18500
10	Si Si	27680
11	Textile Sortir	72000
12	Walkin Boots	86500
13	Way Ahead	12750
14	Grand Total	304430

To filter out particular sets of data, you can use the **Page Fields** area. For example, to see data related to a specific Start Date, drag this field to the Page Fields area. Clicking the arrow allows you to select a particular date and then display that information only.

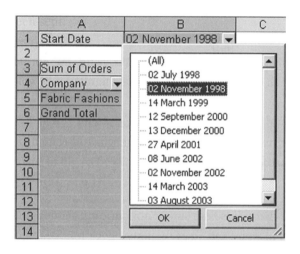

Calculations

The default function is Sum, to show totals. If you want to display the maximum or average prices, however, double-click the cell showing the type of calculation being performed and select an alternative from the list.

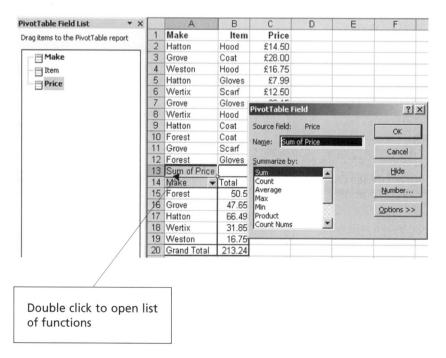

Double click to open list of functions

To display the data differently, you could drag the *Make* field off the *Row* fields area and replace it with the *Item* field, and then change the function to show the average cost of each item of clothing.

13	Average of Price	
14	Item ▼	Total
15	Coat	37.17
16	Gloves	9.38
17	Hood	16.87
18	Scarf	11.50
19	Grand Total	19.39

To see average prices of items by manufacturer, you could now drag Make to the **Column Fields** area and produce a far more detailed display.

Average of Price	Make ▼					
Item ▼	Forest	Grove	Hatton	Wertix	Weston	Grand Total
Coat	39.50	28.00	44.00			37.17
Gloves	11.00	9.15	7.99			9.38
Hood			14.50	19.35	16.75	16.87
Scarf		10.50		12.50		11.50
Grand Total	25.25	15.88	22.16	15.93	16.75	19.39

Formatting

Format your data using the normal font and number formats, or click the *Format Table* button on the *Pivot Table* toolbar and apply an overall design.

CHARTS

To create a chart from data in a spreadsheet, always select the data and column headings (but not total or title rows) and then use the shortcuts and wizards to make the task straightforward.

To create a column chart instantly, select the data and press function key F11. To work through the wizard, make your selection but now click the toolbar button and follow the steps.

Step 1 – select the appropriate chart type

Step 2 – check or change source data

Step 3 – add titles and labels and add or remove the legend (key)

Step 4 – position the chart on the same or a new sheet

Font types and sizes, numerical formats, line styles and background colours can all be changed – either right-click or double-click the element to be offered the formatting options or select any object and use the normal toolbar buttons or options from the **Format** menu.

Having created a basic chart, there are several aspects that you may want to modify. To return to any steps in the wizard, or add missing items, right-click in the chart area or select an option from the **Chart** menu.

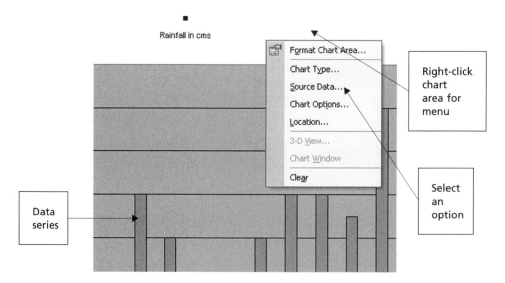

Change chart type

Select **Chart Type** as above and you will be offered Step 1 of the wizard. Select a different chart type from the list and click *OK*.

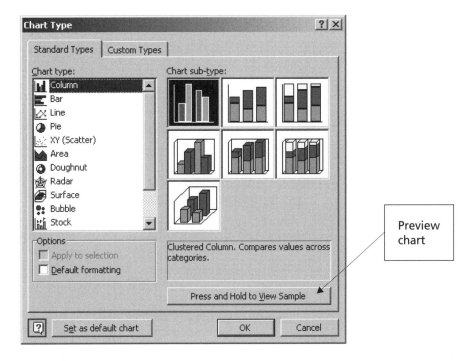

Add labels

Select **Chart Options** to return to Step 3 of the wizard. You can now complete any missing titles and also add pie chart labels – e.g. display a percentage or both label and value.

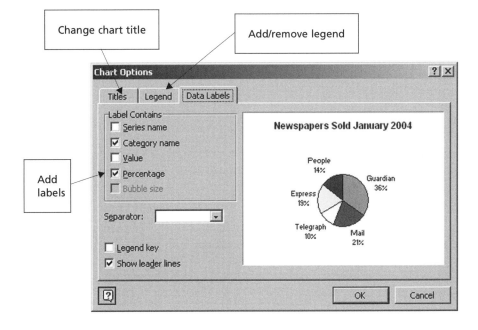

Scale

The wizard will set appropriate maximum and minimum values for your chart but if you want to amend these, select the Y axis, double-click for the **Format** dialog box and click the *Scale* tab.

Having changed your top and bottom figures, you may also need to amend the interval i.e. Major Unit value to display the data appropriately.

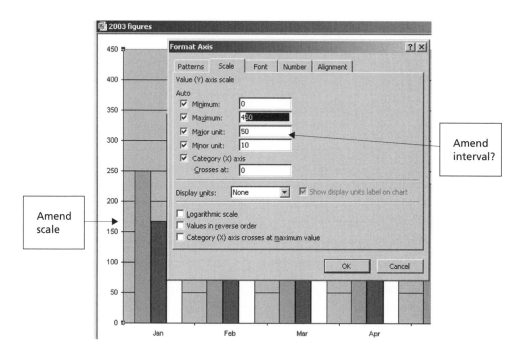

Change data

Once you have created your chart, you may want to amend the data that is being displayed. To make a change without re-creating the chart, select the Source Data option to return to Step 2 of the wizard.

To view your data in different ways, you can show the data series in rows or columns. The labels will form the legend.

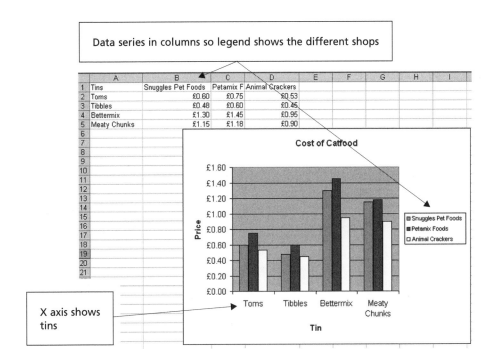

Data series in columns so legend shows the different shops

X axis shows tins

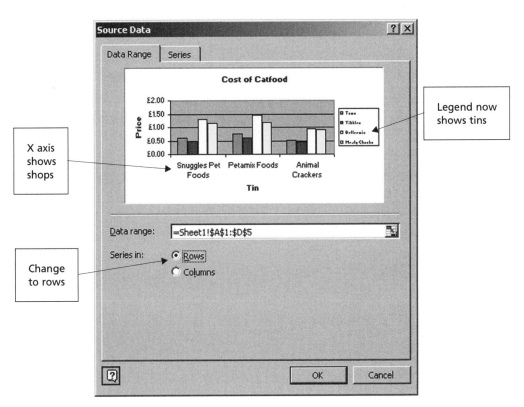

Legend now shows tins

X axis shows shops

Change to rows

A common problem is when axis labels are numerical e.g. years or measurements, as these are often interpreted as a data series. Click the *Series* tab, select the axis that is wrongly included in the Series box and click *Remove*.

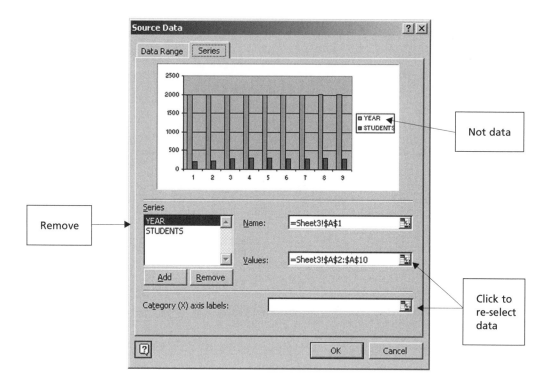

If any labels or values are not displayed correctly, or you want to change the actual entries selected, click the button in the correct box to return to your spreadsheet. Select the appropriate cells with your mouse and then click the button again to return to the dialog box and check the display.

To select data from non-adjacent columns, hold down Ctrl as you drag across the second and subsequent range of cells.

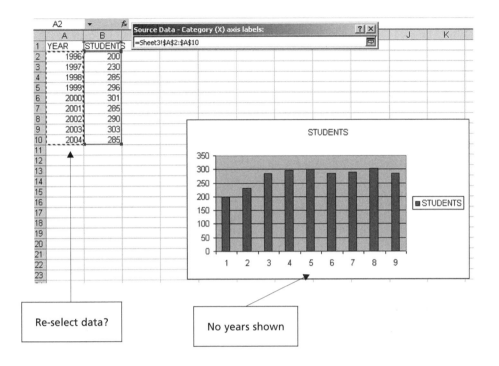

Re-select data?

No years shown

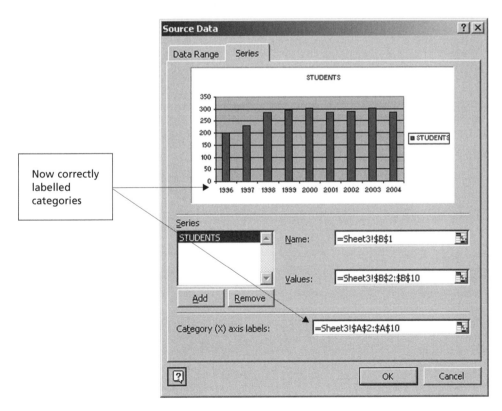

Now correctly labelled categories

Trendlines

On XY scatter graphs, you can add a trendline by right-clicking any point. There are various options available including displaying the equation on the graph.

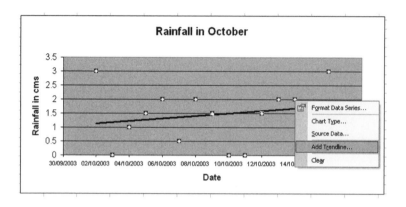

Formatting lines and markers

Where your line chart is comparing data, it is important that you can differentiate between the lines easily. Printing in colour will help, but in many offices your printout will be black and white. To help read the chart, double-click the line or right-click and select *Format Data Series*. You can now re-colour a line or marker, change the marker type or size or remove it altogether.

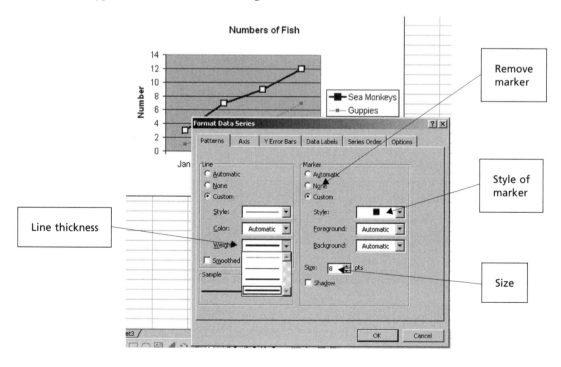

Printing charts

If a chart is on its own sheet, clicking the *Print* button will print out the chart showing on screen. If, however, you have placed your chart on the same sheet as the original data, you must select the chart to print it alone. Otherwise, both data and chart will print together. There is an option available in the *Page Setup* box labelled *Chart* if you want to set the printer to print in black and white: this will help distinguish the different data series.

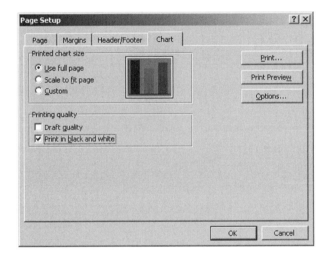

If you want to add your details to a chart printout, use the header or footer option available from the **View** menu. It works as in *Word* except that you need to click the *Custom* button to open the header or footer box.

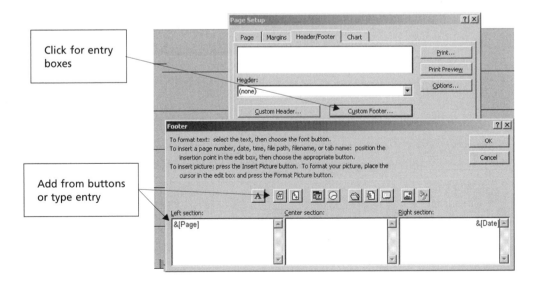

5

Relational Databases

Databases can be small or vast collections of records – depending on the business of your organisation they could include information on anything from staff salaries to buildings, meal ingredients, exam results, stationery suppliers or wallpaper samples.

In the previous chapter you will have seen that spreadsheet packages can be used to create quite adequate databases, but for more sophisticated management of data and the ability to link different sets of records, you are likely to find yourself using a relational database such as *Access*.

There are three main tasks that you may be asked to perform:

1. Input data and keep records up-to-date;
2. Analyse the records to find those meeting certain criteria; and
3. Present the records attractively in the form of reports.

A BRIEF OVERVIEW

A database file can include any number of records, which can themselves be grouped into different tables. For records to be included in the same table, the data must be stored under the same headings, the Field names.

For example, a training department may have a *Training* database that contains the following records: staff attending the courses; course details; locations of the training centres and information on all the trainers. In *Access*, this would mean the database should contain information held in four separate tables: *Attendees, Courses, Venues* and *Trainers*.

The advantage of using a relational database is that information does not need to be duplicated. If, for example a member of staff attended a health and safety course that had the code HS14, details of the course would be held in the *Courses* table and not repeated in the *Attendees* table. Once the tables were linked, it would be possible to search both tables and discover the names of everyone attending the Health and Safety course, their department, the length of the course and the name of the trainer.

Attendees Table

Name	Department	Course Code	Date
Swannic, G	Marketing	**HS14**	August 2004
Bell, P	Advertising	WP2	June 2003
Havering, D	Finance	S12	July 2003

Courses Table

Course	Course Code	Trainer	Length	Town
Word Processing	WP1	Mary Hart	1 day	Bradford
Health & Safety	**HS14**	**Doug Weller**	**2 days**	**Manchester**
Word Processing II	WP2	Mary Hart	2 days	London

PRIMARY KEY

To prevent confusion, as well as allow tables to be linked, one field has to contain data that uniquely identifies the records and this field must be included in all linked tables. In the above example, the training courses must have different codes to distinguish between them all. To preserve this uniqueness and warn anyone trying to enter a new course into the table with the same code that another one already exists, the course code field in the Courses table would be designated as the primary key. You would only need to set primary keys if you were creating a table yourself, but understanding why they have been set may help you if problems arise when you try to enter duplicate data or search linked tables.

ENTERING AND AMENDING RECORDS

Opening the database file reveals a window that stays open all the time. The tabs explored in this chapter are labelled *Tables*, *Queries*, *Forms* and *Reports* and every time you work on an object within the database, you need to first click the correct tab.

To view the records in any table, double-click the name on the *Tables* tab or select the name and then click the *Open* button. (If you need to amend the design of a table, you must click the *Design* button and will see just the fields under which data is stored.)

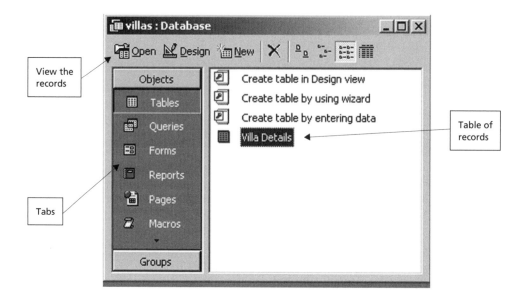

Tables look similar to spreadsheets, but you can only add a new record at the bottom of the table where you will see a pen symbol in the row header area. Enter details for each record across the row, moving with the tab or arrow key. If a primary key has been set, you must complete entries for a full record before you can make any amendments.

To make changes, click any entry and delete or insert text in the normal way. If you want to delete a complete record, select it by clicking the grey row header box and either click the *Delete* button on the toolbar or use your keyboard. If a column is too narrow, click and drag the right-hand boundary between field names or double-click the line to adjust to the longest entry.

Field properties

Occasionally, you may want entries e.g. in a Price field to show decimal places but these don't appear when you type the entry. This is because the table designer has not set the number format correctly. The answer is to click the *Design* view button. You

View table design

Drag to resize column

Delete selected record

Microsoft Access

File   Edit   View   Insert   Format   Records   Tools   Window   Help

Villa Details : Table						
REF	NAME	COUNTRY	SLEEPS	MID	HIGH	LOW
C14	CAPRI	SPAIN	4	£595.00	£875.00	£395.00
L21	LOS ALIMENTA	SOUTH OF FRANCE	4	£695.00	£975.00	£550.00
N34	NATHAN	ALGARVE	4	£725.00	£950.00	£495.00
A12	ACROPOLIS	CYPRUS	4	£795.00	£1,395.00	£750.00
C9	CASA CHAT	SPAIN	6	£795.00	£1,895.00	£725.00
S4	STELLA	CYPRUS	6	£875.00	£1,350.00	£750.00
C7	CASA FAMILIA	ALGARVE	6	£895.00	£1,595.00	£550.00
M12	MARCO POLO	ALGARVE	8	£950.00	£1,775.00	£575.00
E5	EL SOLAZ	MALLORCA	6	£975.00	£1,795.00	£595.00
L10	LAS PALMA	MALLORCA	4	£995.00	£1,650.00	£625.00
B7	BON NUIT	SOUTH OF FRANCE	8	£995.00	£1,495.00	£695.00
A2	AKAMAS	CYPRUS	8	£1,250.00	£1,895.00	£950.00
C24	CAN CAN	MENORCA	6	£1,275.00	£1,995.00	£675.00
M18	VILLA MARTIMA	MENORCA	8	£1,495.00	£2,295.00	£750.00
M21	MARIA	IBIZA	8	£1,550.00	£2,750.00	£750.00
J11	JASMINE	SOUTH OF FRANCE				

Click box to select record

Add new record here

will see just the field names and the type of data they can contain e.g. whether the field entries are text, dates or numbers.

For each selected field a lower Properties box opens where you can make changes to the settings. Click your *Prices* field name and then move down to the properties and change the entry in the Field Size box from Long Integer (the default that will only display whole numbers) to Double. Now you can set the number of decimal places in the Decimal Places box and, when you save the new design and return to your records, future entries will reflect these changes.

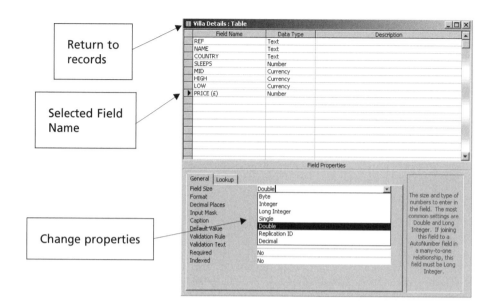

REPLACING ENTRIES

When you need to replace entries in databases holding hundreds of records, finding the correct entry can take some time. You therefore need to use the **Edit – Find and Replace** facility that is available.

To find an entry, type it in the *Find What*: box, making sure you select the correct match: the whole field or only a part.

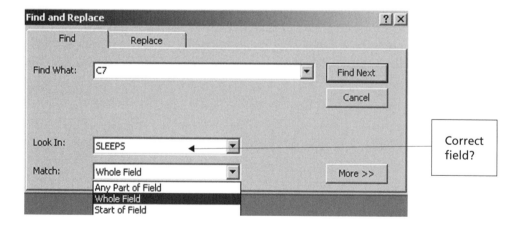

One problem with the *Access* find facility is that only single fields will be searched by default. If you left your cursor marking an entry in the wrong field, click the drop-down arrow in the *Look In*: box and change the entry so that you search the complete table, or return to the table and click the correct field before using *Find*.

To replace entries, click the *Replace* tab and complete the *Replace With*: box. Either click *Find Next* to check by eye before replacing entries, or click *Replace All*. Take care, though, as any changes to your records cannot be reversed easily, and you may make a costly mistake if you replace 1,000 records with the wrong data.

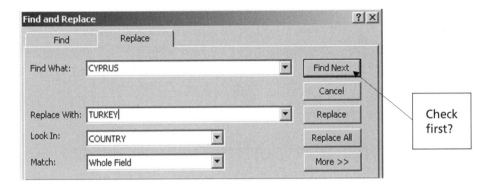

SORTING RECORDS

It is very quick to sort your records alphabetically or by different criteria e.g. from highest to lowest price or earliest to latest dates. Click any entry in the selected field and then click the A–Z (lowest to highest/alphabetical) or Z–A (descending) button on the toolbar. You do not need to select all the data first as records will not be split.

REF	NAME	COUNTRY	SLEEPS	MID
M12	MARCO POLO	ALGARVE	8	£950.00
C7	CASA FAMILIA	ALGARVE	6	£895.00
N34	NATHAN	ALGARVE	4	£725.00
A12	ACROPOLIS	CYPRUS	4	£795.00
S4	STELLA	CYPRUS	6	£875.00
A2	AKAMAS	CYPRUS	8	£1,250.00
M21	MARIA	IBIZA	8	£1,550.00
E5	EL SOLAZ	MALLORCA	6	£975.00
L10	LAS PALMA	MALLORCA	4	£995.00
C24	CAN CAN	MENORCA	6	£1,275.00
M18	VILLA MARTIMA	MENORCA	8	£1,495.00
L21	LOS ALIMENTA	SOUTH OF FRANCE	4	£695.00
J11	JASMINE	SOUTH OF FRANCE		
B7	BON NUIT	SOUTH OF FRANCE	8	£995.00
C9	CASA CHAT	SPAIN	6	£795.00
C14	CAPRI	SPAIN	4	£595.00

Re-ordered records sorted alphabetically by country

FORMS

Very often you will be asked to add or amend records viewed on screen one at a time, rather than within the complete table of data, although the table will be updated automatically with any changes you make. This is because a different object, a form, has been created for you to use as an alternative way to amend records. Forms can be easier to use and may also protect the full table from being viewed by others or changed by mistake. For example, the form may not display all the fields in the underlying table so that only certain entries can be accessed and changed. If no front-end menu has been created, you will find your form if you click the *Form* tab in the database window.

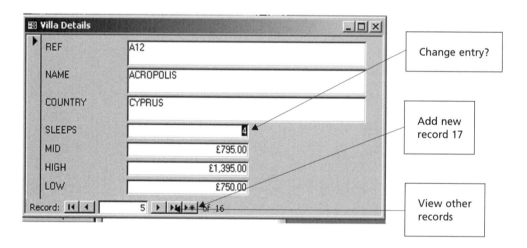

SEARCHING

To identify everyone in your database who retired in 2004, who works from home, who lives in Birmingham or who owns a car, you will need to carry out a search. The structure of the search, which can be saved and run again in future, is known as a *Query* and is based on matching your search criteria with the contents of the fields in your table.

There are four decisions to make when designing a query:

1. *Which fields will you be searching?* For example, you could search the TOWN field for *Birmingham*, the RETIREMENT DATE field for *later than 31/12/03* or the CAR OWNERSHIP field for *Yes*. It is very important that you use accepted

wording, operators or numerical expressions if *Access* is to carry out the search successfully. There are a wide range of accepted expressions you can use when searching a database in *Access*. Here are a few of the most common:

◆ To match any text entry e.g. **Birmingham**, type the word exactly as it appears in the table

◆ To find words beginning with a letter or number, type it plus an asterix * for the unknown characters e.g. **B*** will locate Birmingham, Brighton and Bournemouth. Use the * for any unknowns e.g. to find any numbers *containing* 46, type ***46***.

◆ To find dates *after* 1st May 2004, type **>1 May 2004** and for *earlier* dates, type **<1 May 2004**

◆ For numbers or dates between two e.g. 7 and 15, type **Between 7 and 15**.

◆ To find objects costing more than £2,500, type **>2500** (no £ or comma) and less than £2,500 type **<2500**. For objects that cost £2,500 or more, you need to type **>=2500**

You will notice that, after entering your expression, quote marks appear round text, # symbols round dates but nothing round numbers. These symbols show that the expressions are recognised by *Access*.

2. *What information do you want to see when the records are found?* You can decide whether to display the first name, surname and full address of everyone living in Birmingham, or just their surname and telephone number.
3. *Do you want the records displayed in any particular order?* If so, you need to sort them when you design the query.
4. *How do you want the query saved?* Always name it carefully, so that it is clear what information will be displayed next time you run the same query to carry out a new search.

(You may not be involved in the design of large databases, but you should be aware that some fields could be indexed to speed up searching. Discuss this with the IT experts if you have problems carrying out lengthy searches.)

Designing a query

Here are the steps to take to search a Villa Details table for villas that sleep 6 or more people:

1. On the *Queries* tab, click *Create Query in Design View* having first made sure your underlying table of data is closed.
2. In the window that opens, select the table you want to search and click *Add*. Then click the *Close* button to close the *Show Table* window. If you click Add twice and two Field list boxes appear, select one and delete it or you will end up with very odd results.

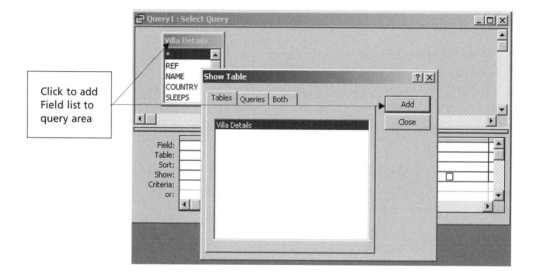

Click to add Field list to query area

3. Decide which fields to view when your records are found. Drag each one onto the grid in the lower window, or double-click to add them automatically. You can also click the next Field box on the grid and then click the arrow to select from the list of fields displayed. If you click the table name above the field list, all the fields will be selected. Drag one if you want to add them all to the lower grid.

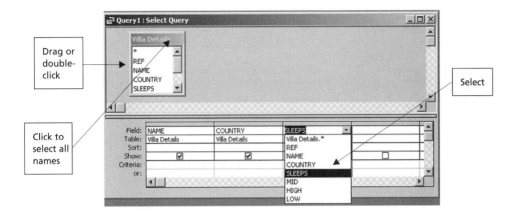

4. To search for villas that sleep 6 or more people, the expression in the SLEEPS field needs to be entered as **>=6**. This must be typed at the bottom of the correct field column in the Criteria row.

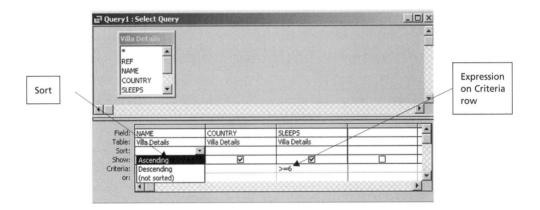

5. To re-order the records, click the field on which to base the sort e.g. alphabetically by NAME and select ascending order.
6. To view the matching records that should now be found, you can either click the *Run* button or *Datasheet view* button on the toolbar.

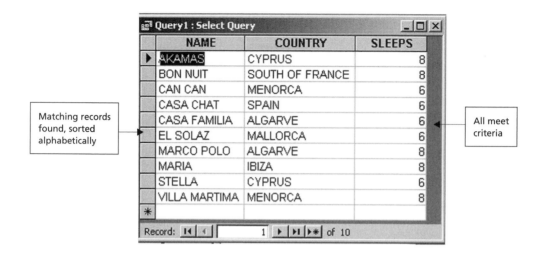

Matching records found, sorted alphabetically

All meet criteria

7. If you don't want to see the entries in the SLEEPS field, you can hide the display by clicking off the tick in the *Show* box. However, the field *must* be included on the Field row as it is your search field.

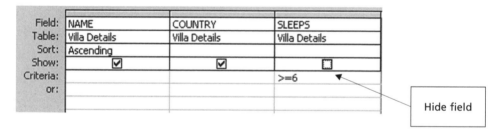

Hide field

SLEEPS field no longer visible

8. If the query doesn't seem to be correct, you can return to the design by clicking the Design view button 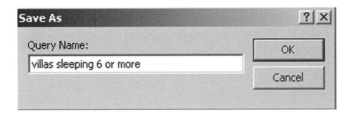 . Check that there are no spelling mistakes or other errors before running it again.

9. When you are happy with the query design, click the *Save* button and give your query an appropriate name. You can close the query and it will be saved on the *Queries* tab.

Regular searches

One common task might be to search your database on a regular basis e.g. to find contacts from various companies, clothes made of different materials or villas in various countries.

For a conventional query, you would need to design a new one every time the criteria i.e. the name of the company, material or country changes. You could then have a range of queries labelled 'Cyprus Villas', 'Portuguese Villas', 'French Villas' etc.

An alternative is to leave the name of the company or country blank, but type an instruction in square brackets into the Criteria row instead e.g. [which country].

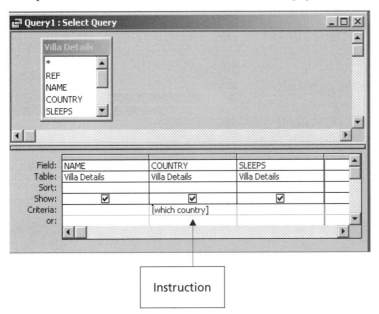

Instruction

Whenever the query is run, a box appears with the instruction to enter the unknown criteria – the parameter value. After typing in a country, the query will run normally and appropriate records will be displayed.

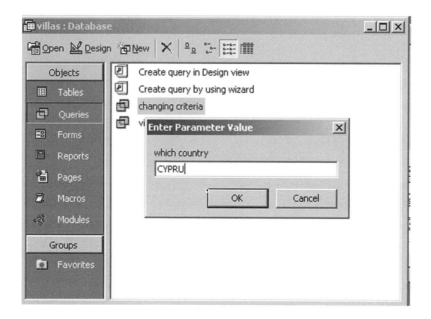

REPORTS

When printing an *Excel* database, you format the cells and print out the appropriate section of the spreadsheet. In *Access*, instead of changing the look of the table, you create a new object known as a Report. This can either include all the records in the full table or can display limited records based on a query.

Reports created automatically

For a quick report, you can use the *AutoReport* feature. On the Reports tab, click the *New* button and select an *AutoReport* style from the list. In the bottom window, select the table or query containing the records you want to display and click *OK*.

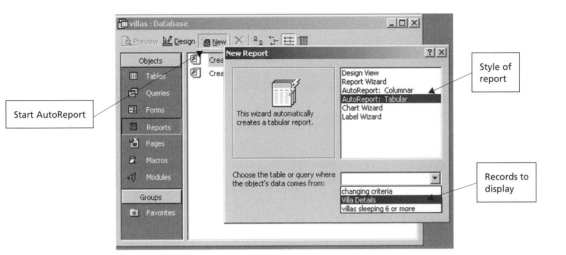

Start AutoReport

Style of report

Records to display

Wait a few seconds and a report will appear.

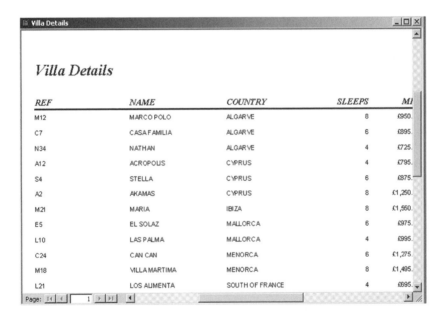

Reports using the Wizard

To have more control over your report, you need to design it step-by-step using the Wizard. This option is available on the Reports tab so double-click to start.

Step 1: Select the table or query on which to base the report and then choose which fields to include. The double arrow will add them all in the original order, but you can select fields one at a time and click the single arrow to add them to the right-hand pane.

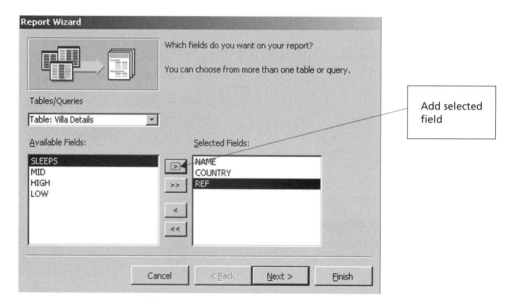

Step 2: Select a field if you want your records grouped in any way e.g. by country, company, year etc.

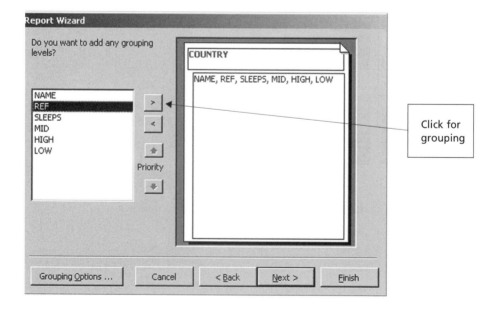

Step 3: As well as a sort option at this stage, you can also introduce calculations. Click the *Summary Options* button and choose to total, average or display maximum or minimum values in any relevant field.

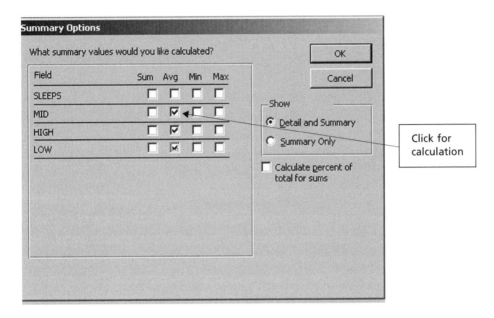

Steps 4–5: Set the orientation of the page and a preferred layout and appearance.

Finally, give your report a name and click *Finish* for a preview.

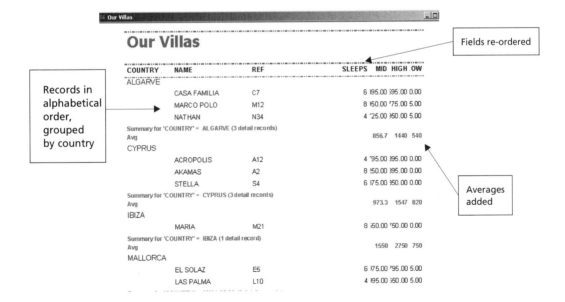

Customising a report

You can see fairly quickly that there is a great deal wrong with the above report. Some columns overlap, unnecessary wording has been added, some data has been lost and the prices have not been formatted to currency.

Fortunately, all these things can be corrected by clicking the *Design* button and going into the design of the report.

Controls

There are two main types of object in a report which are known as controls: the labels e.g. making up the title or headings, and the text boxes that contain data drawn from the database. Controls can be resized, moved and formatted so that, where required, you can give the entries more space and re-position headings and columns of data in the report. To drag controls, you need to move the mouse around until the pointer displays a black hand 🖐 .

Click the *Aa* button on the toolbar to draw a new box if you need extra labels anywhere on the report. You may need to de-select the control and then click it again to access the formatting buttons on the toolbar.

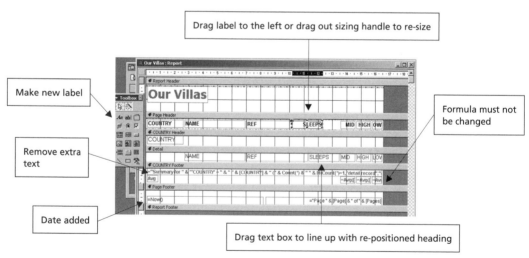

Delete unwanted labels by clicking and then pressing the *Delete* button. For example, you can remove the date and page number codes added by default as well as the text starting *'Summary for'* & *'COUNTRY'* . . . You can also amend the label *Avg* to something more meaningful such as *Average Price*. However, it is important to leave the actual formula **=Avg[(MID)]** intact.

Click the Preview button to check the changes you are making.

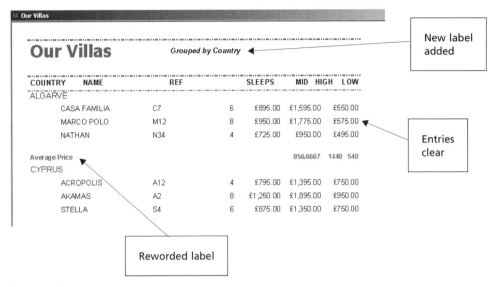

Format data

If you want to format e.g. numbers to currency or change the number of decimals showing, you need to right-click a text box control in the *Design* view and select *Properties*. Click in the *Format* box and select an alternative such as Currency from the list. You can then set the decimal places to a new number before closing the properties box.

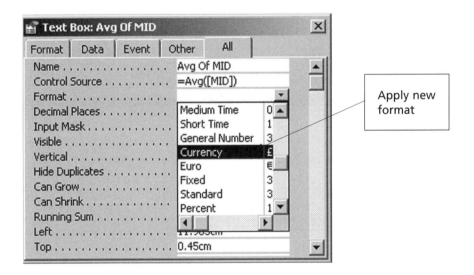

LINKING TABLES

To search two or more tables, these must first be linked. For a link to be possible, both tables must contain the same field containing the same type of data. In one table it is the primary key field but in the second table it is referred to as the foreign key field as duplicates are quite acceptable. The second table would also have its own primary key field.

Imagine you have the following two tables of data: one contains details of your contacts in various companies and the other details of all your meetings. The structure of the tables would appear as follows:

Contacts table	*Meetings table*
Contact ID (Primary key)	Booking code (Primary key)
First Name	Date
Surname	*Contact ID* (Foreign key)
Position	Location
Company	Time

Adding a primary key

If you are creating a table, you can add the primary key to any field in *Design* view. Select the field in the *Field Name* list and click on the key symbol. Save this change and then return to your records by clicking the *Datasheet* view button.

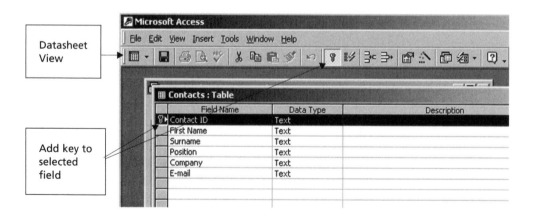

To link the tables, you must click the *Relationships* button on the database window after clicking the *Tables* tab.

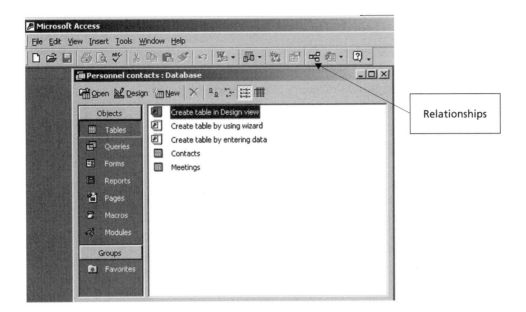

Add all the tables you want to link from the *Show Table* window and then locate the primary key field in one table (where it will appear in bold). Click its name and then drag it to drop over the foreign key field in the second table. A window will open showing the type of relationship and you can leave the default settings. Click *OK* and you will see that a dark line has appeared showing that the link has been made.

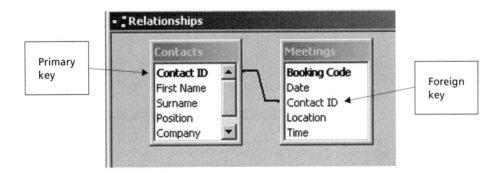

Save the changes and now, when you want to search across the tables, you can add both to the *Query* box and continue setting up a query exactly as you have done for a single table search. The Table row automatically shows which table each field comes from.

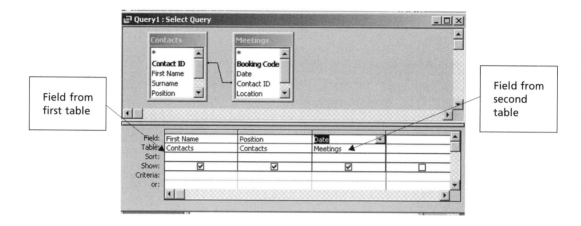

Field from first table

Field from second table

COPYING DATA

Access offers three quick ways to copy your data into other applications: you can create a text file in *Word*, a spreadsheet in *Excel* or initiate a mail merge again in *Word*.

Word processing

Select the table name on the database window, click the arrow next to the *Office Links* button and select *Publish It* with *MS Word*.

Office Links

Wait a few moments and *Word* will open showing your table of data on the page. As the file is in a rich text file format (simpler than full *Word* formatting), you may prefer to save it with a new name as a *Word* document. Treat the data just like any *Word* table. (Sometimes the table is too big to fit on the page: if so, you may prefer to open the *Access* table, select and copy the data and paste it into *Word* in one or more blocks.)

Spreadsheets

Select the *Analyse It* option and your data will appear in a new *Excel Workbook* where you can treat it exactly as normal *Excel* data.

Mail Merge

Selecting the *Merge It* option will either open a blank *Word* document that displays the *Mail Merge* toolbar along the top of the page or will link the data to a file you can find on your computer. All the fields from your table will be available from the *Merge Field* button so that you can create a mail merge document directly. (Details in Chapter 3.)

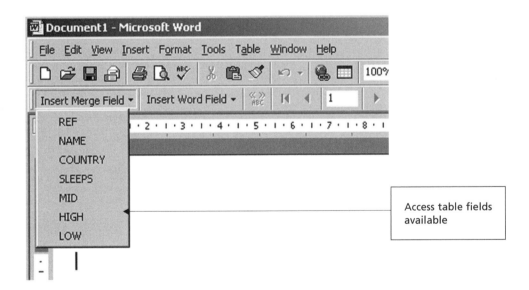

Access table fields available

IMPORTING DATA FROM ELSEWHERE

One very important task may be to combine or use data that is stored in non-*Access* applications such as *Excel*. You therefore need to know how to import data into *Access*. There is a wizard to help you, and you move through the steps by clicking *Next*.

1. Create a new database or open the destination file and click the *Tables* tab.
2. On the *File* menu, select *Get External Data – Import*.

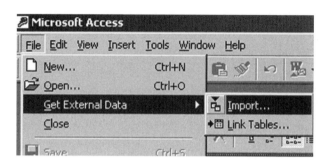

3. When the *Import* window opens, make sure you search for appropriate files e.g. *Excel* spreadsheets or CSV (text) files. When the file is visible, click it and click *Import*.

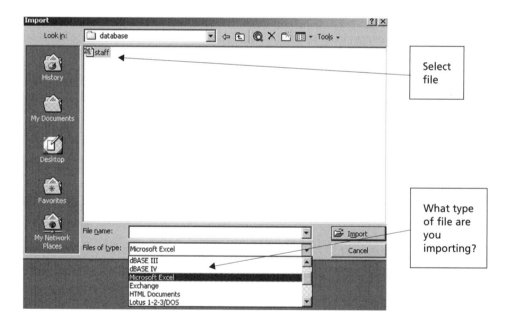

4. When the relevant data appears, check that the column headings (new field names) are shown against a shaded background. (Before importing, it is a good idea to check that the column headings form the first row of the spreadsheet or other data file. If necessary, remove any titles and empty rows as you will otherwise end up with the generic field names Field 1, Field 2 etc. created by *Access* and will have to rename them yourself.)

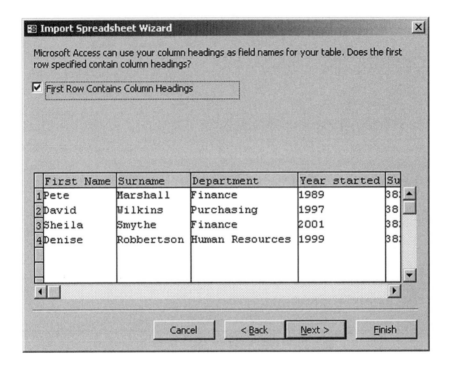

In the next window, select the appropriate option – to add the records to an existing table selected from the drop-down list or to create a new one. If adding records, you must be sure the field names in the table and spreadsheet are the same or the process will not work.

You will be offered the option to delete or rename some of the fields and remove or change the primary key field. Finally, name any new tables before finishing the importing process.

Your new table will now appear in the database window.

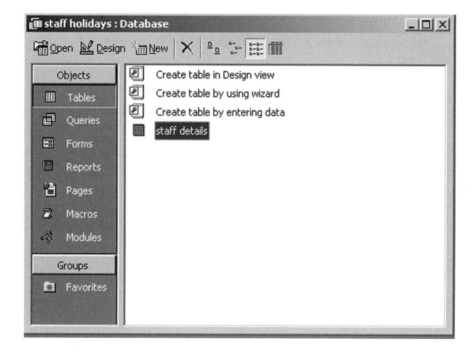

6

The Internet and World Wide Web

The Internet, for those of you who have not yet connected to it at home or at work, is the name given to the networks of computers that allow machines to communicate with each other across the world. The two main uses you are likely to make of the Internet at work are to send and receive electronic messages (e-mails – covered in the next chapter), and to view pages of information.

These pages – web pages – make up the World Wide Web and can contain text, pictures, sounds or video clips. Most organisations nowadays publish their own Websites (a collection of linked web pages) to provide visitors with details of their products and services, and one of your tasks may involve keeping some of these pages updated. Programs known as content managers enable companies to manage their Websites and you will be trained in their use if you are asked to carry out this type of work.

Most of your time on the Web will probably involve using it as a vast encyclopaedia, finding specific information such as telephone numbers, contact addresses or locations of companies, carrying out research, checking prices, reading reports or even following an online training course. In some areas of work, material may be made available by practitioners in the field that you are welcome to make use of without charge, and there are sites where you can ask for advice or guidance on a wide range of technical and non-technical topics.

One disadvantage that comes with so much information now being available is that you may have to spend time each week or month keeping yourself up-to-date. Many organisations will no longer inform you by letter or in the press that changes have taken place to relevant legislation, syllabuses, systems or financial data but you will still be expected to be aware of the current position.

DOWNLOADING

Any web page that appears on your screen is actually saved temporarily onto your computer through a process known as downloading, but a further function of the Internet is to allow you to download whole programs that you might need to help you work more effectively. These are often made available at little or no cost by manufacturers or software companies. Your employer may be unhappy about you downloading programs as they can take up a large amount of space and can also be a way to introduce viruses, but sometimes it may be necessary if a utility is required. People commonly download file readers, trial image editing programs, up-to-date software controlling equipment such as digital cameras or scanners, the latest anti-virus software or an enhanced web viewer.

INTERNET V. INTRANET

Just to confuse you, there may be two different networks that you can connect to: the Internet and a smaller, local network known as an Intranet that is only available internally to members of staff. Intranets have now replaced the conventional notice board and newsletter as a way to keep staff up-to-date with developments within the organisation, and you will probably only be able to access it fully at your desk.

THE BROWSER WINDOW

The software that allows you to view web pages is called a browser, and you will usually find an icon for one of the two main browsers: *Internet Explorer* or, less commonly *Netscape*, on your desktop. You will probably find that your organisation remains connected to the Internet most of the time, so that opening the browser will download a web page straight away without any need to connect manually. If that is not the case, click a *Connect* button that will appear to first make the connection.

If you are new to the Web, the following image introduces the main elements of the view offered by your browser:

Links to pages within the same site, or on other relevant Websites, are built into each page, and your mouse pointer changes from an arrow to a hand whenever it is over a link. Clicking the hand will open the linked page. As you are likely to move backwards and forwards over a large number of web pages when searching for information, use the buttons on your toolbar to go back ⬤ through the pages or move forward ➡ again, or return to your starting point, called your home page, by clicking the Home button ⌂.

SAVING WEB PAGES

When you find useful information that you want to store, you can click the *Print* button to print out a hard copy or you can save the page onto your computer by selecting **File – Save As**. Decide if you want to store the whole page including any image or sound files that are associated with it, just the page you see on your screen or simply the textual content, and choose your options from the *Save as type*: box.

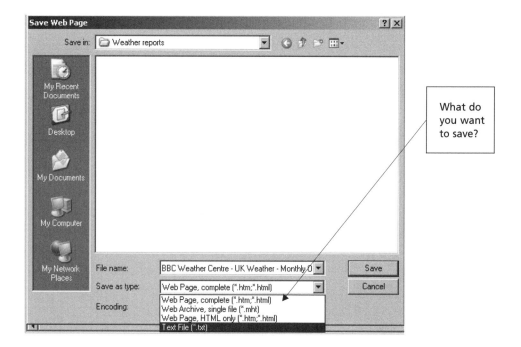

SAVING PICTURES

To keep a copy of a photo, drawing or other image found on a web page that is not protected by copyright (which would prevent you using it without permission in any publications), right-click and select *Save Picture As* before saving as normal.

WEB ADDRESSES (URLs)

Web pages created by any organisation that has a Web presence are stored on dedicated computers and have a specific address known as the URL (Uniform Resource Locator). These computers may be provided by the organisation itself or they may be made available by a 'hosting' company. As each page has a specific address, typing this into your address box and pressing *Enter* or clicking a *Go* button will locate the page and download it onto your computer.

The address of any web page is made up of several parts:

http:// denotes that it has been published on the Web using accepted protocols; these characters appear automatically without you needing to type them into the address box;

www. shows that it is on the Web and the letters are included in most, but not all web page addresses;

bloggs.co.uk is the *domain* name, which includes the registered name of the organisation and an extension that indicates what type of business it is;

/products/laptops/mini.htm (or **.html)** indicates the individual web page you are viewing, showing its location within sub-folders on the Website and that it is written in Hypertext Mark-up Language (HTML) code.

Usually, when searching for information on the Web you will type in the general Website address e.g. www.bloggs.co.uk which will take you to the opening or welcome page. You can then use indexes or search boxes provided on the page to locate the actual piece of information you are looking for.

If you do not know the exact URL but want information about a company, educational establishment or charity etc., URLs follow certain conventions so the address is likely to take the form:

www.name.**co.uk** *(British company)*
www.name.**com** *(International company)*
www.name.**org.uk** *(charity or public body)*
www.name.**gov.uk** *(local or national government)*
www.name.**ac.uk** *(British university or college)*
www.name.**edu** *(American educational establishment)*

BASIC INFORMATION WEBSITES

As you gain experience searching for information, you will discover some Websites that are particularly useful. As well as the Websites of named organisations that you would obviously visit first of all for information about their own products or services, there are many sites that provide general types of information. Here are a few that I return to many times:

www.yell.co.uk – an online 'Yellow Pages' site for finding company details
www.streetmap.co.uk – find and print out a map for any postcode or street
http://dictionary.cambridge.org/ – a dictionary to check meanings and spellings
http://asadz.com/thesaurus/ – alternative words for written work

www.howstuffworks.com/ – clear explanations for how most technical, computing and increasingly other things work

www.netdoctor.co.uk – medical advice and information

www.nationalrail.co.uk/ – for planning any journey by train

www.bookbrain.co.uk – search for the cheapest copy of any book

www.kelkoo.co.uk – compare the prices of items such as cameras or computers

SEARCH ENGINES

When you don't know where to start in your search for information, you need the help of a type of Website known as a Search Engine. A button labelled *Search* on your Internet Explorer browser toolbar will offer MSN Search, but you may prefer to visit another site. These sites all hold vast databases of web pages and either match these to your chosen 'keywords' or provide more limited links to web pages classified under various headings and sub-headings.

At the present time, the most popular search engine is www.google.co.uk but there are many others that people like to use such as www.yahoo.co.uk, www.altavista.com, www.megaspider.com (that lists search engine sites), www.ask.co.uk or www.hotbot.com.

They work as follows:

1. On the opening screen, decide whether you are looking for a web page, a picture or want to work through a category listing and click the appropriate button or tab.

2. For normal Website searches, type your search criteria into the search box, being as specific as possible to make sure you don't get an endless list of barely relevant web pages.

   a. For example, if you need to find suppliers of mosaic tiles to add to craft packs you are putting together for a promotion; don't simply type 'tile suppliers'. Make sure you include words such as 'UK' (or click a UK checkbox if available), 'mosaic', 'hobby' or 'craft' etc. before searching to cut out foreign suppliers or swimming pool or roof tile companies from the search list that will result.

   b. Link two or more words inside quote marks to search for the full phrase e.g. 'Handel's Water Music' displayed a list of 3,700 web pages whereas 17,000 were listed when the three words were typed separately.

   c. Type a complete question if you are unsure which key words to use, as the search engine will simply ignore extraneous words such as 'and', 'in' or 'that' and will still find relevant pages for you to visit.

3. Press *Enter* or click the *Search* or *Go* button to display the list of matching web pages. Each web page link displayed should show a little of the page contents, the URL or the date it was last updated. This will help you decide if the site is worth visiting.

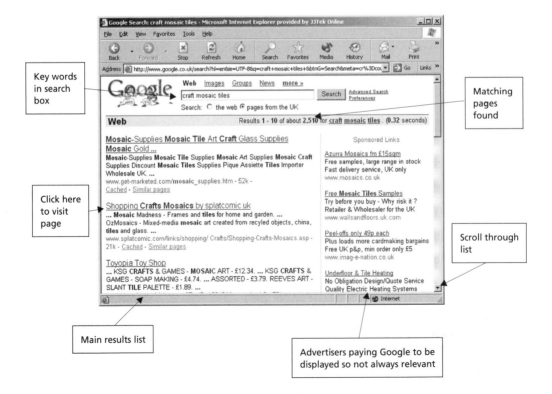

4. Scroll down and click any titles to visit that particular page. Use your Back button to return to the list if the chosen page is not worth pursuing.

Finding the information

Some pages can be quite densely written, so that finding the particular data you are searching for is hard. Get help from the **Edit** menu by selecting **Find (on this page)**. You can now jump from entry to entry matching your key words until you come to the appropriate section.

Directory search

For a category/directory search (e.g. *more> - Directory* in Google), click the top level heading and work down through the sub-headings you are offered. You will end up with a limited number of web page links to follow up.

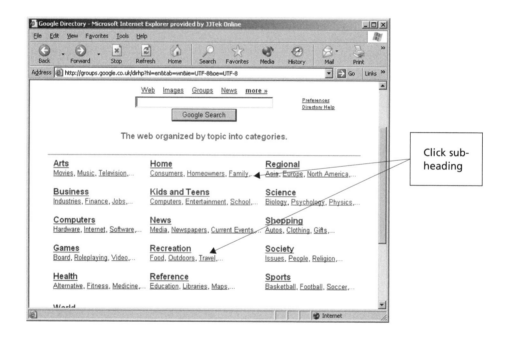

FAVORITES

Having searched successfully for information, you may end up viewing a page that you would like to refer to again in the future. Save time by storing a link to the page in the filing system within your browser – *Netscape's Bookmarks* or *Internet Explorer's Favorites* – so that you can re-visit the page at any time by opening the folder and clicking the URL.

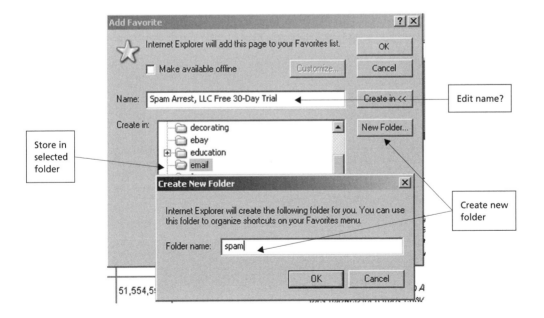

Adding

Some folders will already have been created in the Favorites menu, but add the URL of an open web page to the end of the list by holding Ctrl and pressing the letter D. Later, you can file it or just drag it to a new position on screen using the mouse.

To organise your ULR links more sensibly, click *Add to Favorites*. This opens a dialog box where you can file your new URL in an existing folder by clicking it in the list, or create a new one for it by clicking the *New Folder* button.

Change the entry in the *Name* box if it is too long, and click the *Make available offline* box if you want to store a copy of the page and view it in future without connecting to the Internet.

Visiting

To visit the page at any time, open the Favorites list in your browser window, open the selected folder and click the *URL*.

Organising

To re-organise your favourite links, you can right-click them on screen and select *Delete* or *Rename* from the menu. Otherwise, click *Organize Favorites* from the *Favorites* menu. In the window, locate any URLs and click the appropriate button e.g. to move them to different or new folders, rename or delete them altogether.

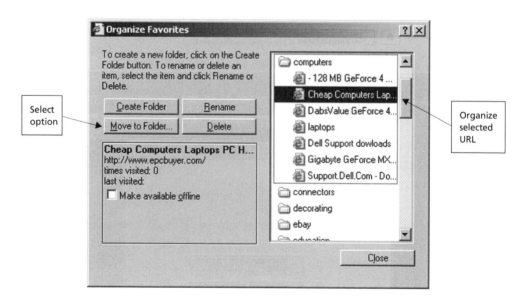

HISTORY

Sometimes, you visit a site earlier in the week, cannot remember much about it but know you want to visit it again. This is where the *History* function is so useful. Clicking the toolbar button  will open a menu showing exactly which Websites you visited during the past few weeks. Click any day and you should be able to retrace your steps and find the recently visited page.

Click to view URLs visited that day

VIDEO CONFERENCING

Some years ago, a meeting in Coventry, Clapham or Cincinnati could entail long train or plane journeys and perhaps overnight accommodation. Nowadays, you can talk to those same people from your desk by means of a video conference which, in many instances but not all, involves using the Internet.

Although not yet in common use, video conferencing may be something you have to help organise or take part in – perhaps for a training session or to talk face to face with customers or colleagues in other parts of the country. It is therefore useful to know what is involved.

How it works

Video conferences take place either between individuals at desktop computers or in a specially equipped room where members have to gather together at a set time. Participants need a video camera, microphone and speakers that are usually mounted on a computer. As someone speaks at the distant location, you will see a live image of them. Their voice is carried over the network and received by your speakers, and images generated by their video camera appear in a window on your monitor. The system also allows you to work on documents together, sharing files or using a whiteboard.

There are various networks that can be used for transmitting sound and images: local networks; Integrated Services Digital Network (ISDN) phone lines that are usually specially installed; or the Internet. Here communication may be via a normal telephone line, Asynchronous Digital Subscriber Lines (ADSL) or Broadband. Video conferencing uses compressed digital images, but at least a 128kbps connection (the bandwidth) is needed if the quality is to be of an acceptable standard.

Problems

Major difficulties occur when trying to hear people at the remote site if they are not near the microphone, or see them if they are seated at the periphery of the group or in a room that is poorly lit. In a dedicated room, it is therefore important that chairs, cameras and microphones are adjusted and tested so that the optimum conditions for video conferencing are achieved.

You may also suffer the annoyance of broken connections if using phone lines that drop out, and there is occasionally a slight delay in transmission so that you may miss a speaker's first few words.

7

E-mails and Diary planning

Many organisations have adopted *Outlook* as their e-mail and diary management system, but you may come across alternatives such as *First Class* or *Eudora* that work in a similar way. Although there are many sophisticated tasks that can be performed, here are the major functions you will need to master:

◆ Maintaining the Calendar of appointments and meetings
◆ Setting up to-do lists using Tasks
◆ Writing yourself Notes – an electronic version of post-its
◆ Keeping an address list of Contacts including group mailing lists
◆ Sending and receiving e-mails
◆ Working with attachments
◆ Managing your messages

When you open *Outlook*, you have a choice of screen display: the *Outlook Bar* offers large icons and the *Folder List* has a simpler display. Retain at least one of these panes – available from the **View** menu – to allow you to move around easily as you just click any folder to reveal its contents in the main window.

Whichever folder is selected, the *New* button will create a relevant object e.g. with the Inbox selected you open a new e-mail message window but with the *Calendar* selected you can create a new appointment.

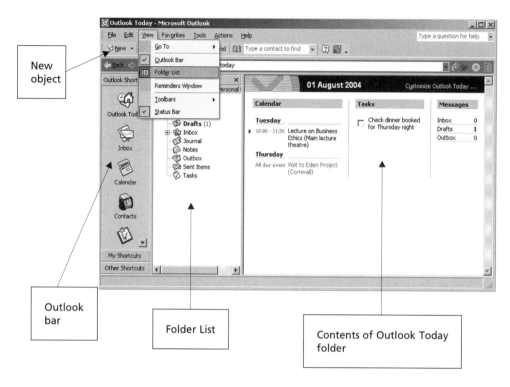

New object

Outlook bar

Folder List

Contents of Outlook Today folder

To amend the general settings within *Outlook* e.g. deciding the times when the Calendar day starts or finishes, what colour your notes will be, or how e-mails should be formatted, open the **Tools** menu, click **Options** and change the relevant settings from the **Preferences** tab.

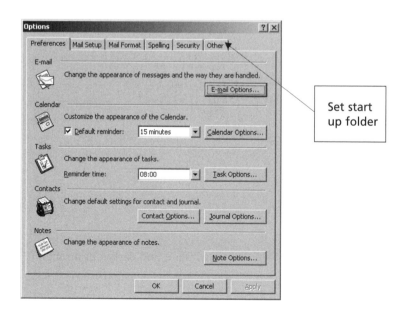

Set start up folder

Start up

If you have a full diary and will be juggling appointments, tasks and e-mails, it can be a good idea to start *Outlook* with the *Outlook Today* folder open. This offers a summary of the week. However, if you mainly work with messages, start up with the Inbox open to display your e-mails. Change which folder opens when you start up *Outlook* by selecting the **Other** tab and then clicking the *Advanced Options* button.

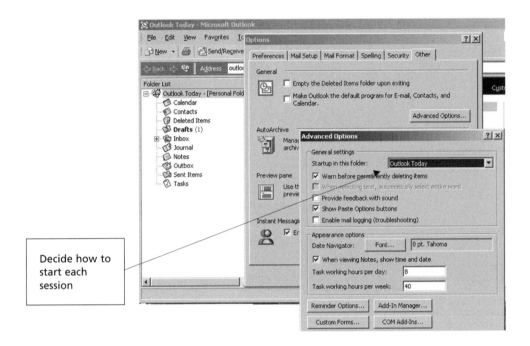

Decide how to start each session

Relationships

You will find that the objects within *Outlook* are interchangeable, so that if you want to remind yourself of a task, for example, you can drag it to the Inbox to create a new e-mail message or turn e-mails into tasks by dragging them in the opposite direction. You can also drag messages to the notes folder to create a 'post-it' reminder. People can be invited to meetings by e-mail at the same time as you are setting up the meeting details, and information in an e-mail can be turned into an appointment if the message is dragged to the *Calendar* folder.

Each type of object will have many unique features in the creating window, but you can usually change any display via the **View** menu and carry out a range of activities via the **Actions** menu.

THE CALENDAR

Views

Display one day, week or month at a time by selecting your preferred view from the toolbar. (Right-click the toolbar if any button is not visible, click *Customize* and drag up the button with your mouse.)

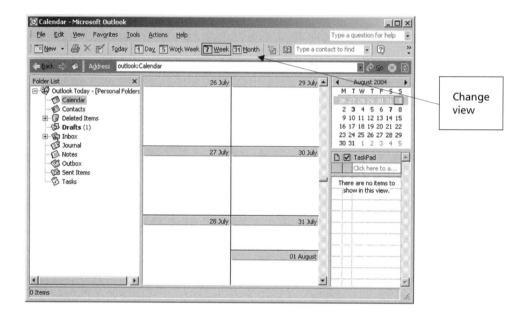

Appointments

The Calendar objects you can create are Appointments (where actual times can be set); Meetings (to which you can invite attendees); and Events (all day appointments with no time slots). They are all based on the same template and can be created by double-clicking the appropriate day in the main window, or clicking the *New* button.

In the window that opens, change from *Event* to *Appointment* by clicking *off* the tick in the *All day event* box. Time slots will appear and you can set the date, time and subject of your appointment by completing the boxes, as well as add any extra information you want to note. The 'busy' box will be selected by default so that others with access to your diary know when you are unavailable.

To hear an alarm or see an on-screen reminder near the time of the appointment – if you will be sitting at your computer – click in the *Reminder* box. A bell symbol will show next to the appointment details when you return to the Calendar. Save the appointment by clicking the *Save* and *Close* button.

To amend the appointment, double-click it in the Calendar to re-open the window.

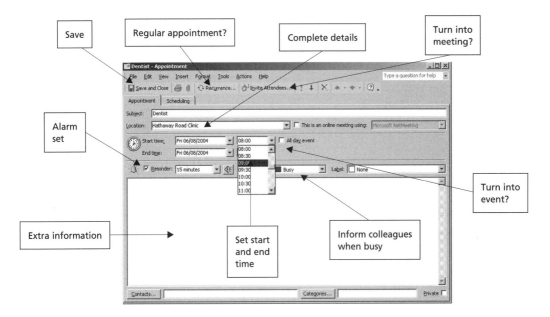

Recurrent appointments

Sometimes you will want to create details of regular appointments. Do this by clicking the Recurrence button and selecting the appropriate options. An end-date after 10 appointments will be set automatically but you can change this if you want them in the Calendar for a longer period. The ⟳ symbol will be visible next to the appointment details.

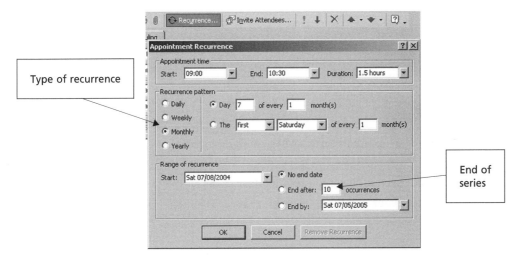

If one of a regular series of appointments needs to be changed, double-click it in the Calendar window and open and amend the single occurrence.

Meeting invitations

When planning a meeting, click the *Invite Attendees* button to open an extra *To*: window. Here you can enter the e-mail addresses of everyone being invited and can send them invitations automatically by clicking the *Send* button.

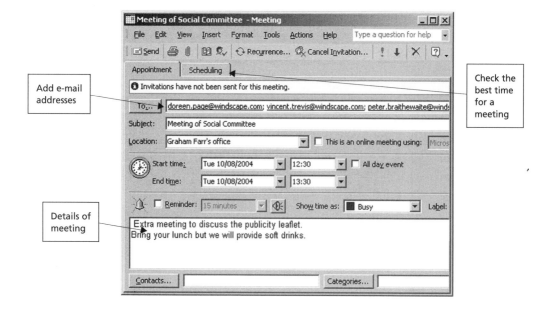

For anyone with access to colleagues' diaries, and only if they always keep these updated, you can also click the *Scheduling* tab to check if everyone is free for the proposed meeting. Drag the boundaries of the meeting to change start or end times if some people are busy.

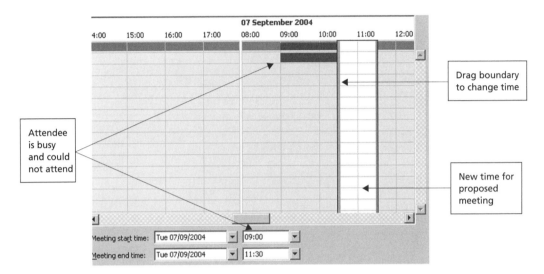

Printing

To produce a hard copy of your Calendar, select the style of printout from **File – Page Setup** and then amend the items to print or formats showing in the dialog box. Click the *Header/Footer* tab to add an entry at the top or bottom of the page and always check in *Print Preview* before printing.

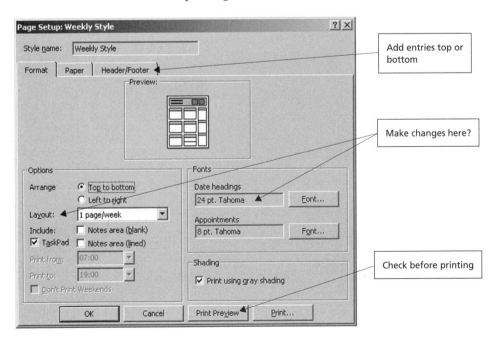

TASKS

Whenever you have tasks to perform and want to keep track of them, you can use the *Tasks* part of *Outlook*. In the 7-day view of the Calendar there is a small *Task pad*, or you can open the *Tasks folder* for a larger grid. Create a new task by typing directly into the grid.

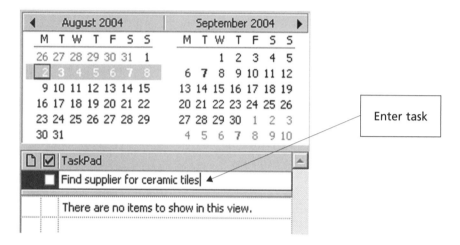

To add further details, click the *New* button or double-click the grid entry. You will open a window similar to the *Appointments* window but will have different options e.g. you can set a completion date, priority and status for the task and even assign the task to someone else via the **Actions** menu.

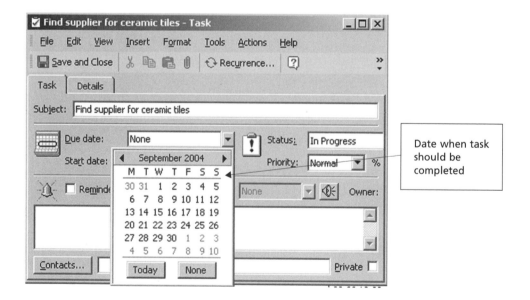

As tasks are completed, they will be shown dim with a line through them in the *Task pad* whereas overdue tasks are coloured red.

In some systems, you may not be able to see your tasks because they have been filtered out. Turn off the filter by going to **View – Current View – Customise Current View**, click the *Filter* button and then click *Clear All*.

NOTES

It is now time to remove all those yellow sticky notes from round your computer! Instead, open the Notes folder and type yourself a note in the label that appears. To keep a reminder more accessible, you can even drag the label out of *Outlook* and onto your desktop.

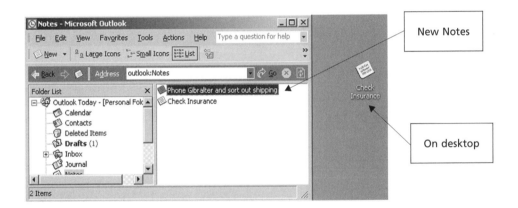

CONTACTS

The Contacts folder is your personal, electronic address book, although your company may also provide access to other address books. As well as keeping e-mail addresses in Contacts, your can also store postal addresses and telephone numbers, and you can recall an e-mail address automatically when creating a new message.

Add an address

To add an e-mail address from someone who has written to you, right-click their name in the *From*: box and click *Add to Contacts*. This will open a new Contacts window where you can complete the boxes. Open this box at other times by selecting the Contacts folder and clicking the *New* button.

You can complete as many boxes as you like, but always include the Full Name to appear in your list of addresses as well as the e-mail address. To re-open the window for editing, simply double-click the name in the main Contacts window.

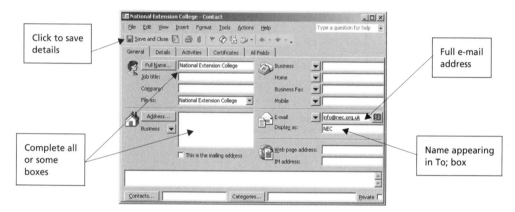

Group (distribution) mailing lists

If you often send the same message to a number of people, you can group their e-mail addresses together and give the collection a name. Use this name whenever you want to add their details to the *To*: box in one go.

1. Click the *Contacts* folder and then click the down-facing arrow next to the *New* button and select *Distribution List*.

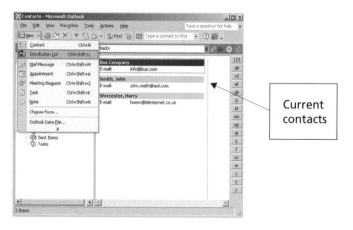

2. In the window, give the group a name and then add e-mail addresses from any address books you are able to access by clicking the *Select Members* button and then selecting the names and clicking *Members*.

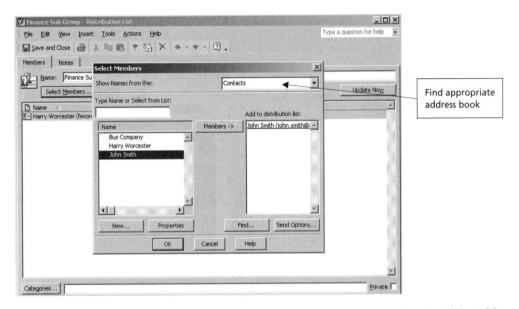

3. For addresses not in your Contacts folder or any global address book, click *Add New* and complete the boxes. Click the *Add to Contacts* checkbox if you also want their details kept separately in your Address Book.

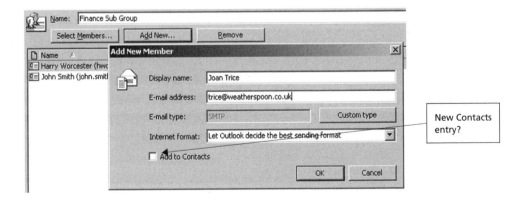

4. When all entries have been added to the group, the name will be displayed in Contacts and you can add it to an e-mail in the same way as a normal address.

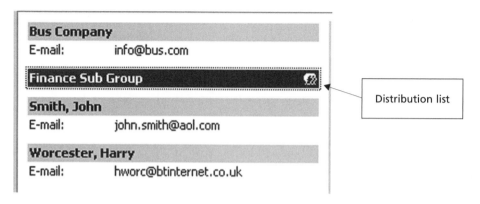

E-MAILS

Addresses

You will normally be given an e-mail address when you start work, which will have the following structure that you type in lower case with no spaces:

	name@domain name
e.g.	jackie_sherman@smallisbeautiful.co.uk
or	j.sherman@ smallisbeautiful.com

When receiving e-mails, the system often displays a name rather than full e-mail address e.g. *Jackie Sherman*, but the address will still be available if you right-click the *From* box and select Properties.

If you receive an e-mail from someone who has the domain name hotmail.co.uk or yahoo.co.uk, take care: it means this is a private e-mail address and, unless freelance or self-employed, they may therefore *not* work for a legitimate business.

Creating messages

E-mails sent to your e-mail address will arrive in the Inbox. To read one, double click the message and it will open into its own window. You may have a preview pane showing where you can also read the message, and you can turn this on or off via the **View** menu.

Click the *Inbox* folder and then the *New* button to create a new message and make sure you always complete the following boxes accurately:

To: the full e-mail address of anyone you are writing to – for more than one recipient, separate their addresses with a semi-colon and always ensure they are typed 100% accurately or the message will not be sent.

Cc: the full e-mail address of anyone receiving a copy of the message

Subject: a brief summary of the contents of the message, so that those you write to can see at a glance whether it is worth opening the message now or later

Main message window: as mentioned in the chapter on word processing, business messages should remain formal in tone although you may find you soon feel able to address people by their first name rather than using the conventions of Mr. or Mrs. as in business letters.

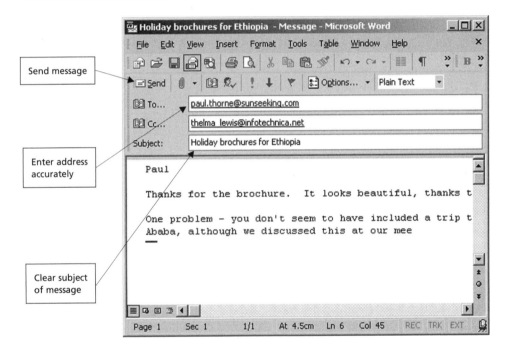

If you are always online, clicking the *Send* button will send the message straight away. Otherwise, it will be placed in the *Outbox* ready for sending. To retain a message to work on later, click *Save* and it will be stored in your Drafts folder.

For really urgent messages, click the exclamation mark button to add a high priority banner to the message, or find the option from **View – Options**.

Recall address from Contacts

To save time typing out e-mail addresses accurately, click one of the book symbols in the message window. Select the name(s) and click the appropriate button to add them to the correct boxes.

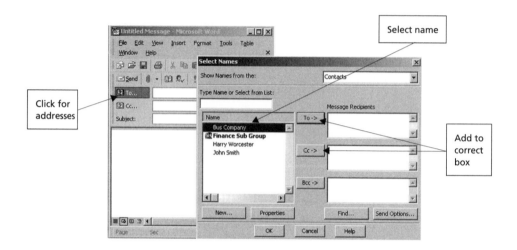

Blind copies for confidential messages

The Bcc box allows you to send copies of your message in secret to other people. It is particularly useful if you want to write to a number of people but *don't* want them viewing each other's full e-mail address. If you address the message to yourself (or leave the To: box blank) but add their names in the Bcc box, all they will see is *your* name or their own at the top of the message when it arrives.

Open the Bcc box when composing a message by selecting **Bcc Field** from the **View** menu.

Responding to messages

When you receive and open a message, you will see buttons labelled *Reply, Reply to All* and *Forward* at the top.

Click *Reply* to send a message to the author of the e-mail only. Boxes containing their e-mail address and the subject of the message, prefixed by *Re:* will be completed already.

Click *Reply to All* only if you want to send your reply to everyone who received a copy of the original message. Otherwise they will all see your comments – which may be of a personal nature!

Click *Forward* to send on the message (and any attachments) to a third person. The box containing the subject of the message will be completed already, prefixed by *Fw*.

Attaching files to e-mails

There are three different ways to attach a file to an e-mail: as you create the message; from the desktop; or from the file itself.

When creating a message

With your message window open, click the paperclip icon labelled *Insert File*.

This opens your computer and you can browse for the file(s) you wish to send. Select one, or hold down Ctrl to select several files before clicking the *Insert* button.

Back in your message, you will see your attached file(s) displayed in a new Attach window above the main message. Each will show the type of file and its size. Remember that anything over 2 MB may take a while to send or to download into your recipient's Inbox, so zip or compress files that are very large (see Chapter 8 for further details of how to zip files).

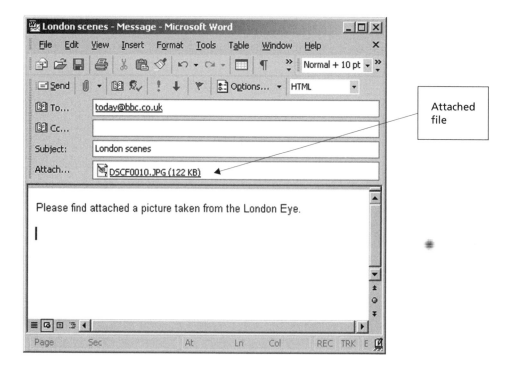

From the desktop

Locate any files you want to send from My Documents, a sub-folder or a floppy disk and right-click to display the menu. Select the *Send To* option and click *Mail Recipient.*

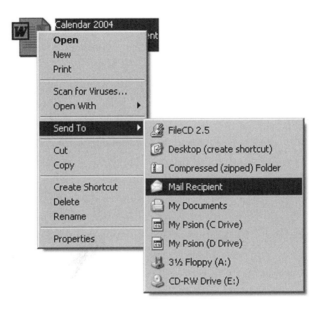

A new message window will open with the file already showing in the Attach box. You will probably need to amend the automatic subject and message details that will appear but can then treat the message as a normal e-mail.

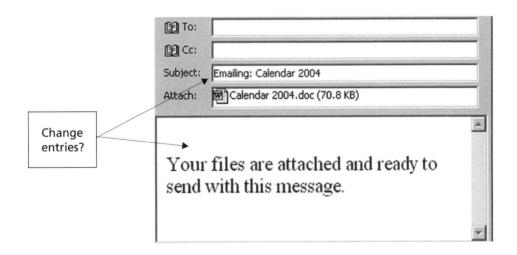

From within an application

If you finish creating a document and decide you want to send it as an attachment, open the **File** menu and click **Send to – Mail Recipient (as Attachment)**. You will once again open a new message window showing the file already attached. Complete the details and send as normal, bearing in mind that you must *not* close the file until your message has been sent.

(There is also a button on most *Office* toolbars 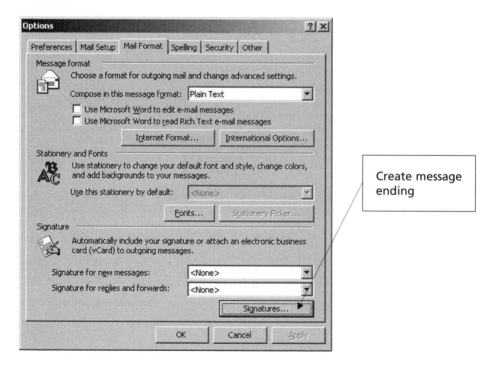 which will offer e-mail headings and will allow you to create a message and send a file as the message text.)

Open an attachment

Double-click the file name showing in the Attach box to open an attachment you have been sent. You are likely to be directed to save it first, in case it carries a virus.

Signatures

Business e-mails often contain information about the sender e.g. full job title, postal address and direct line. To add such details to your messages quickly, create one or more signatures. You can set the system to add this to every message, or select an appropriate signature as and when it is required.

1. Go to **Tools – Options**, click the *Mail Format* tab and then click the *Signatures* button.

Create message ending

2. Click *New* in the window that opens, name the signature, click *Next* and then type in all the details.

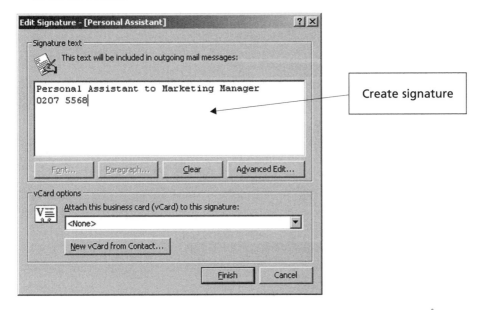

3. Click *Finish*, check the details are correct and then click *OK*. Repeat the process if you have more than one identity and require several different signatures.

4. Make sure you select *None* in the *Signature for new messages*: box if you want to use signatures sparingly. Otherwise, your new signature will be added automatically every time you write a message.

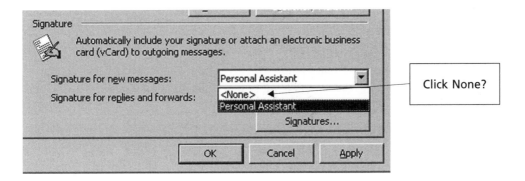

5. To add a signature to a message manually, click at the end of the message text and open the **Insert** menu. Click *Signature* and, if there are more than one, select from the names listed.

Message options

For messages where it is important to know it has been read, you can request a receipt. Open the **View – Options** menu and click in the box for a reply if the message is read.

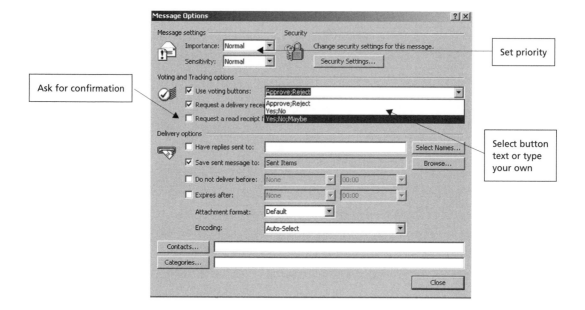

You can also include a voting button if you want people to let you know if they can attend a meeting or if they approve of a plan. Their message will include a labelled button which they can click to send an automatic reply.

Out of Office messages

If you will be away from your desk for a time and want your messages replied to, you can set the computer to send out a standard 'I will be away' holding reply automatically. Do this by clicking **Tools – Out of Office Assistant,** selecting the 'currently out....' option and typing in the message people will receive. If you want a particular colleague to deal with your messages, click *Add Rule* and specify where messages from particular people should be forwarded.

Don't forget to take off these settings when you return by clicking the 'currently in the office' option.

Managing messages

It is easy to allow your incoming messages to fill the Inbox, but this is not only inefficient, in some organisations there is a limit to the number of e-mails you can store. So here are several things you can do to manage your messages:

Delete unwanted messages

◆ If you are keeping messages because they contain useful information such as an address or phone number, first copy the details to an appropriate place e.g. your Contacts. You are then free to delete the message.

◆ For snippets of information, an alternative is to copy the message details into a Note before deleting the e-mail.

◆ To keep the full or partial contents of a message safely, open the **File** menu and select **Save As.** You can then store a copy of the e-mail with related files in your My Documents filing system. A different method is to copy the contents to a word processed or other relevant document – select the contents, right-click, click *Copy* and then paste into your document.

◆ Where messages have attachments you want to keep, save these outside *Outlook*. You don't even need to open the message, simply select it in the Inbox, open the **File** menu and select **Save Attachments**. Find a suitable location for the attachment(s) and click *Save*.

File messages

For messages you need to keep within *Outlook*, make sure you move them out of the Inbox as soon as you can into a suitably labelled folder. New incoming messages will then be clearly visible in the empty Inbox.

Make a folder by right-clicking the Inbox and selecting *New Folder*. Type a name for the new folder and then click *OK*. You can now drag any relevant messages across from the Inbox into the new folder.

Archive old messages

Some messages may need to be kept for months or even years, even though they are rarely referred to. The best way to deal with these is to archive them. This involves setting up an archive file to which your old messages are continually added. The messages are first copied to the archive file and then deleted from your mailbox.

There are three steps to this process:
1. Decide how long to keep messages before they are archived.
2. Set *Outlook* to check the system on a regular basis and move old messages automatically to the archive file.
3. Arrange a link to the archive file so that messages can be retrieved easily.

Decide how long to keep messages

Outlook has default archive settings for many folders e.g. two months for sent messages, but you may want to retain certain types of message longer or shorter than this and will always need to set a time for the Inbox. To select a specific date, open the **File** menu and click **Archive.**

Click the *Archive this folder* . . . button and select the target folder from the list. Now pick a date from the calendar when messages will be moved to the archive.

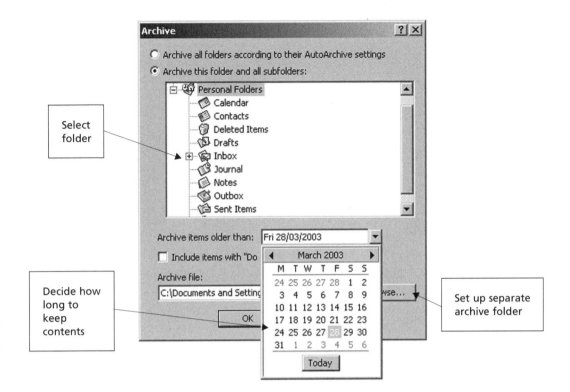

Select folder

Decide how long to keep contents

Set up separate archive folder

The system will set up a default archive file named *archive.pst* within *Outlook*, but you may be asked to create a new one on a different drive. The file is a type known as a Personal Folders File (.pst) and you should give it a name that clearly labels it as an archive file.

You can change the archive settings for any folder from the main *Outlook Folders List* if you prefer by right-clicking it and then clicking *Properties*. Select the *Auto-Archive* tab and click *Archive this folder using these settings*.

If you want to remove old messages permanently, set the system to delete them once they reach the archive age.

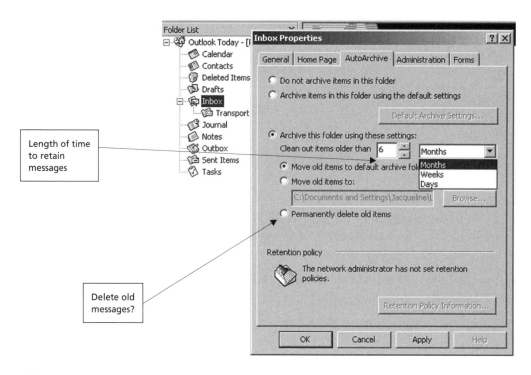

Turn on AutoArchive

To set *Outlook* to carry out the archiving process automatically, select **Tools –
Options** and click the *Other* tab. Click *AutoArchive* and decide when to run the
checking process e.g. every 14 days. You can ask for a prompt on screen whenever the
process is taking place.

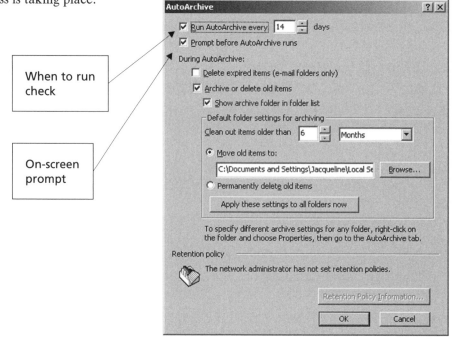

Linking the archive file to Outlook

The archive folder will retain the exact format of your current *Outlook* folders, and you can add it to the Folder List. To see an old e-mail, open the Archive folder and click the relevant *Inbox* or *Sent* folder or sub-folder to display the contents in the normal way.

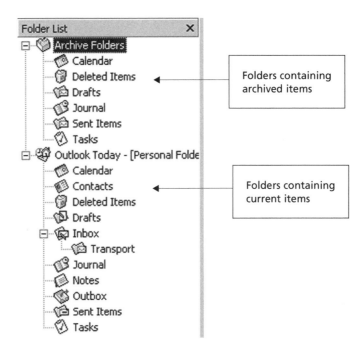

For stand-alone machines, go to **File – Open**, click *Outlook Data Files* in XP machines (Personal Folders File in *Windows 2000*) and select the archive file. When you return to *Outlook*, you will see a new folder labelled *Archive Folders* containing a copy of all your folders. Click the + sign to display a folder and then open the old messages from here.

For networked computers e.g. *Windows 2000* machines, Go to **Tools – Services**, click **Add** and in the *Available information services* window click *Personal Folders – OK*. Locate your archive file and then click *Open*. When you close the window you will see your Archive Folders in the folder list.

Message rules

The most efficient way to deal with incoming messages is to set up rules. For example, you can set Outlook to move all messages from John Smith directly into an Inbox folder labelled *John's Mail* or move anything with 'Congratulations' in the subject box straight to your Deleted Items folder.

To set up rules, open the Inbox and select *Organize* from the **Tools** menu or click the toolbar button [icon] . A window will open above your Inbox messages with various boxes already completed.

If you want to move an individual message without setting up rules, you can use the top boxes labelled *Move message selected below to* . . . Click the message, select the appropriate folder to move it to and click the *Move* button.

You may simply like a quick way to identify certain messages – click the *Using Colours* link to colour particular messages when they arrive in your Inbox.

If you want to create a rule that will move messages from a particular sender to a specified folder each time they write, check that the correct folder name is showing in the box and click the *Create* button.

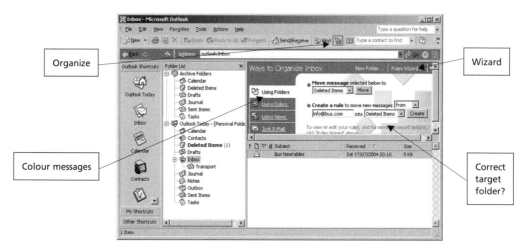

You will be told that the new rule will be applied to all new messages. You can also have the rule applied 'retrospectively' to any messages from the sender presently in your Inbox.

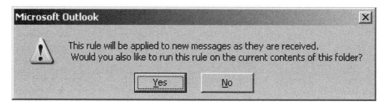

For more complex rules, click the link to the *Rules Wizard*. (You can also right-click a message and select *Create Rule* – this will offer a slightly different route to that set out below).

If you have already created a rule, it will be showing in the window and you can select it and click the *Rename* button to give it a shorter or clearer name, or click *Delete* to remove it completely.

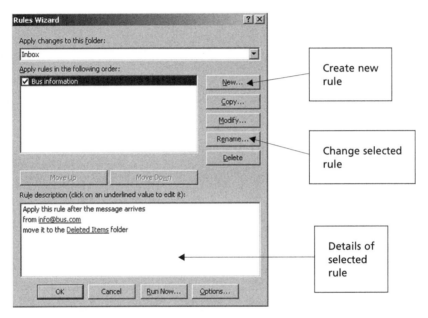

To create a new rule, click the *New* button. You will be offered a range of the most common rule templates you are likely to need, but if nothing is suitable, you can also create your own rule from scratch.

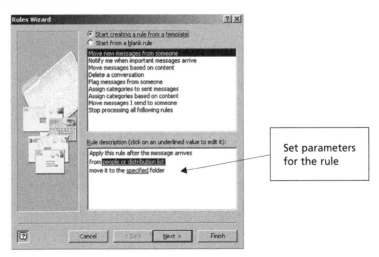

To move incoming messages from someone in your Contacts address book to a named folder, check that the first option in the top window (*Move new messages from someone*) is selected and then click the *people or distribution list* link in the lower window. This will take you to your Contacts where you can select the sender's e-mail address.

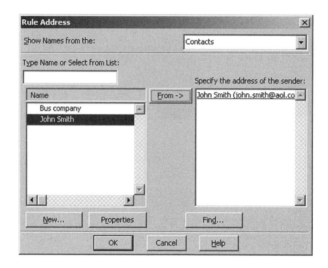

Click *OK* and now click the link to the specified folder. Select it from the list or click *New* to create one at this point.

Back in the Wizard, details of your new rule will now be displayed in the lower window.

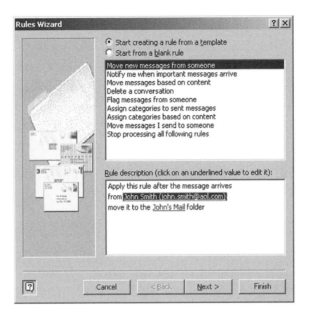

The Wizard now takes you through a series of options that will allow you to add caveats or extra features to your rule before you confirm all the details and give the rule a name. You can also set *Outlook* to move any old messages to their destination according to your new rule.

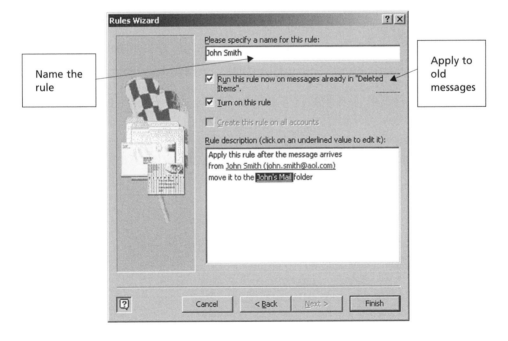

If you receive too much junk mail or any unsavoury messages, either create a rule that moves them to the Deleted Items folder (if you can specify the sender or words in the subject box), or right-click, select Junk E-mail and add them to the appropriate senders list. A new folder will be created within your Deleted Items folder in which the messages will be stored, so that you can check them before they are deleted.

View or edit this list e.g. to remove an address added by mistake, by opening the *Organize* window, click *Junk E-Mail*, then click 'for more options click here' and then click the *Edit* link.

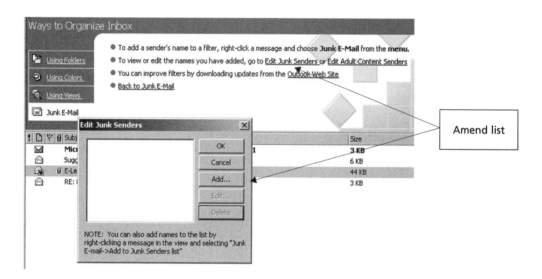

Searching

We all lose messages at some time, so being able to find them again is a useful skill. A quick way is to re-sort the contents of a folder. Re-arrange your messages by clicking the column heading e.g. to organise by name alphabetically or by date received. Each click will reverse the order in that particular field/category.

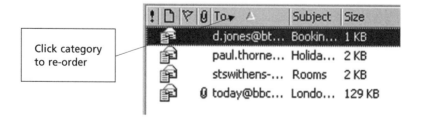

To find messages more systematically, use the *Find* function. Click the button 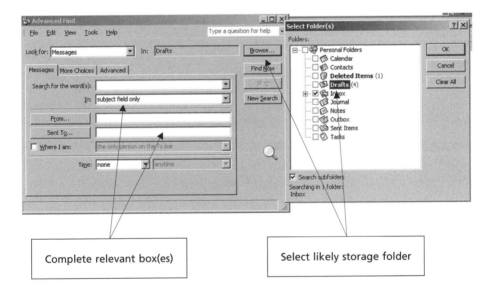 or select the option from the **Tools** menu to open the Find window.

You could use the limited boxes (labelled *Look for . . .* and *Search In . . .*) that will appear, or you may prefer to click **Options – Advanced Find** to search in more detail. Now enter as much information as you can about the missing message e.g. who it is from, the subject of the message etc. and then click the *Find Now* button.

If the probable storage folder is not listed in the In: window, click *Browse* to display all the *Outlook* folders and click the correct folder name. All sub-folders will be searched at the same time.

If time is relevant, you can click in the *Time*: box to select when the message was created or received and limit the settings to options such as today, within the last seven days or last month.

Complete relevant box(es)

Select likely storage folder

After clicking the *Find Now* button, any relevant messages will be displayed in a lower box that will open automatically.

Zipping (Compressing) files

Large files are a nuisance: they won't fit onto a floppy disk and take far too long to send by e-mail. It is therefore a good idea to compress them if you want to work with them more easily.

The process, commonly known as 'zipping', involves creating a folder called an archive and then 'squashing' a copy of the file inside. You can add a number of files to the same archive and then send or save this folder in the same way as a normal file.

The usual requirement when sending an archive by e-mail is that the recipient has a similar program on their computer if they are to extract and read the files inside, but it is also possible to create self-extracting archives when sending files to someone you know does not have the program.

Windows XP machines include their own program that will allow you to compress any files very easily, but with earlier operating systems you will need to install a shareware or freeware program such as *WinZip*. Most employers will be able to provide such a program, but if not, you could download one from the Internet if downloading is acceptable within your own organisation.

USING *WINDOWS XP*

Compressing files
Having found the file on the desktop that you want to compress e.g. in My Documents or a sub-folder, right-click and select **Send to – Compressed (zipped) Folder**.

Immediately, a new folder will appear at the bottom of the list of files and folders displaying a zip and with the same name as the original file.

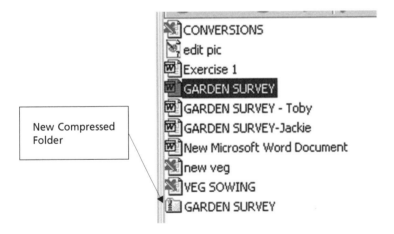

To add several files to the folder, select them all first and then right-click any one and choose the compress option. The folder will display the name of one of the selected files. You could also drag any file into a Compressed Folder to add it directly.

Resizing pictures

When e-mailing pictures, if you click the e-mail link in the task pane but don't first compress them, you will be offered the option to resize them so that they are easier to view. They will, however, be larger than if they were zipped.

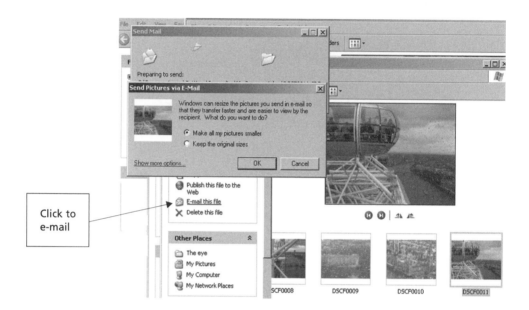

Click to e-mail

Reading zipped files

If you want to view files that have been compressed, double-click the folder. Any file inside can be opened as normal. It will be Read-Only, so you won't be able to make any changes to it directly but can go to **File – Save As** to save a copy to a new location so that you *can* work on it.

You can also use the Wizard to save the files.

1. Select the extract option.

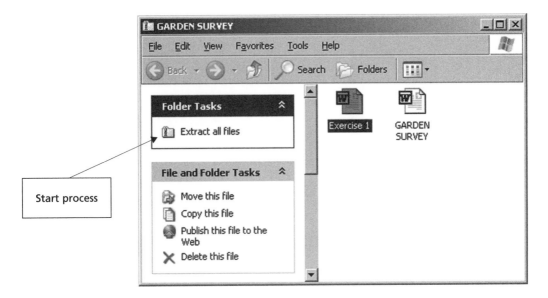

2. Click *Next* to select a location for the files.

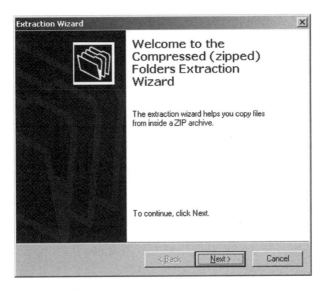

3. Choose the folder in which to store the files by clicking the *Browse* button and, if necessary, create a new folder for them. Then click *Next* for the extraction process to be completed.

4. When all the files have been extracted, click *Finish* and, if you selected this option, view the files in their new location.

USING WINZIP

A version for evaluation purposes can be downloaded from www.winzip.co.uk and you may like to set it to open in Classic mode. Depending on the version you have, the screen may look slightly different.

Creating an archive

If you want to zip one file or have grouped several files into the same folder, select the files and then right-click and select the quick option to zip them into an archive with the same name. Otherwise, follow the guidance to create and store the archive folder and then add the files manually.

Double-click the program icon on your taskbar ![taskbar icon] or open from the **Start – Programs** menu. Click the *I Agree* button to start using the program.

Click the *New* button to create the folder.

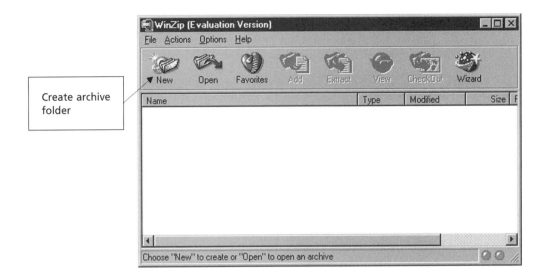

Create archive folder

As it will only contain compressed versions of files already on your machine, you are unlikely to want to keep the archive permanently. Make it easier to work with by naming it carefully and storing it temporarily somewhere accessible like your desktop.

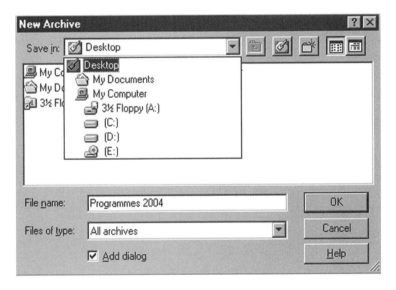

Adding files

After clicking *OK*, you will open the *Add* window. Browse for the files you wish to add and select them in the window. To add more than one file to the archive, hold *Ctrl* as you click subsequent files before clicking the *Add* button.

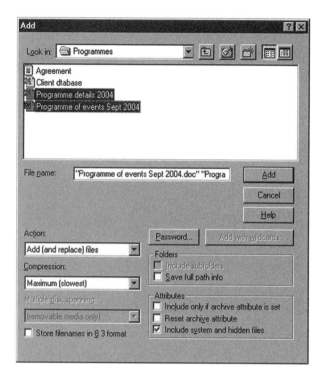

When you have added all the files, close the *Add* window. You will return to the archive and will see the contents listed in the window. You could click the *Add* button to add further files if necessary or just close the window.

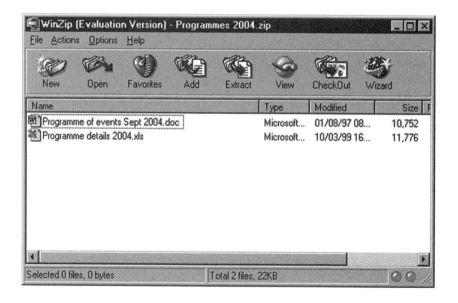

Your archive will now be visible and you can send it as an attachment just as you would a normal file.

Reading zipped files

If you receive an archive, double-click it and you will see the zipped files listed in the window. Double-click any of these to read. If you want to keep copies, save each one separately or click the *Extract* button to save a large number of unopened files quickly. To extract only selected files, click these first. Browse for the folder in which to store the files and click *Extract*.

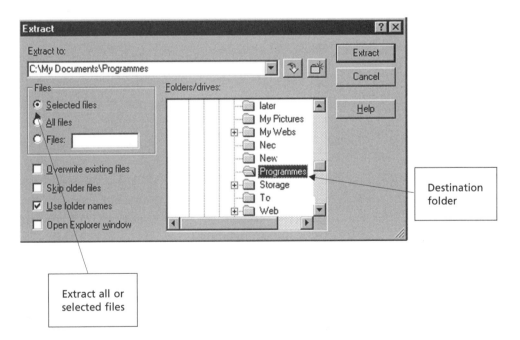

9

Digital Cameras

Unless you plan to work for a photographer, you may be wondering why you need to learn about digital cameras when preparing for a new job. However, here are just a few situations where it can be helpful to have mastered photography on a computer:

◆ Taking photos of new members of staff, award ceremonies, company premises, celebrations or visits by VIPs for internal newsletters or promotional material;

◆ Adding photos of equipment to a manual;

◆ Editing important but poor quality photos taken by others that need to be sent out e.g. to clients by e-mail;

◆ Manipulating images added to personnel records or taken for security purposes;

◆ Helping students or creative members of staff who use photography in their courses or media-related work;

◆ Submitting photos to the webmaster managing your organisation's Website.

THE BASICS

Memory

Some digital cameras found in the office may still be storing images on floppy disk, but this is now very rare. Instead, they will use a range of removable storage media known as memory sticks or cards. These can be any size but commonly range from 16 MB – 128 MB which means they can hold anything from 10–80 photos. The great advantage of digital cameras is that, as they do not use film, the same memory card can be wiped and used over and over again.

Resolution

Camera resolution is the technical term for the quality of the pictures you can produce, and is measured in dots (or pixels) per inch. The higher the resolution (e.g. produced by a top quality 5-megapixel camera), the larger the pictures that can be printed whilst retaining their quality, but that should only be a worry if you have to use an extremely cheap camera and want to print very large pictures.

Taking pictures

Unless you are very interested in photography, you can produce perfectly adequate pictures by simply using the automatic focus and settings on your camera to 'point and shoot'. Most cameras have dials that you must set to still photography, video or preview mode, depending on what you want to do. As long as previous users have transferred their photos to a computer, you should have plenty of room for yours and just need to ensure that you have spare batteries handy, if you are going to keep the camera switched on for more than an hour or so at a time.

Your camera will allow you to preview pictures as you work, so that unwanted images can be deleted straight away, but if you have room it is simplest to transfer them all onto your computer and then work with them here.

Transfer can be directly via cables connecting your camera to a USB port (the common connection point for equipment), there may be a docking cradle or, if your organisation owns a range of different camera types, you may need to remove the memory card and insert it into a universal reader.

Image file types

Digital cameras commonly store photographs in a compressed format known as a JPEG file. However, you can save images in other formats and you may come across TIFF files (e.g. for scanned images), GIF – used for simple, reduced colour drawings and animations, and bitmap images created using *Microsoft Windows*. Image editing software supports a wide range of file formats and some even produce their own e.g. *Paint Shop Pro's* PSP files that make the most of their special features.

For pictures on the Web or sent by e-mail, it is recommended that you to stick to JPEG and GIF.

ON THE COMPUTER

You may have one of a number of image editors on your computer that you can use to view and edit your pictures. Software is normally included with the camera, but your organisation may well have installed one of the more powerful programs such as

Paint Shop Pro (used as our example) or *Photoshop*. Most tend to offer very similar features for basic editing.

Whatever program you use, you should be able to carry out the following main tasks:

◆ View the pictures
◆ Save pictures onto your computer
◆ Clear the camera's memory
◆ Cut out unwanted sections
◆ Rotate an image
◆ Add text
◆ Improve colours or sharpness
◆ Organise pictures to print out

Viewing pictures

The best way to view your pictures is to open the image editor and then select **Browse** from the **File** menu. Make sure your camera is switched on and its contents will be revealed (although you may have to search for it in the folders list) as it is interpreted as an extra drive, similar to your CD-ROM drive or floppy disk drive. Your pictures will be displayed as thumbnails and you can double-click any one to open it fully on screen.

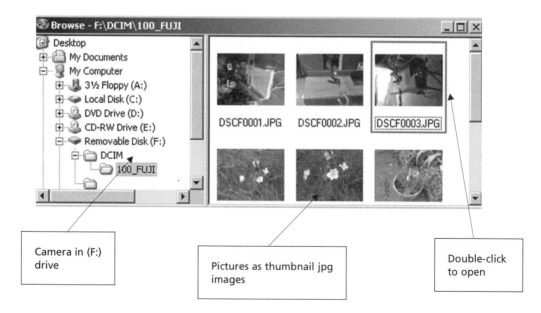

Camera in (F:) drive

Pictures as thumbnail jpg images

Double-click to open

Saving

The pictures will have been saved with default names such as DFC0004.jpg that will mean nothing, so at some stage you should open any you want to keep, go to **File-Save As** and save them with sensible names into appropriate folders on your computer. You could also right-click and select *Copy to* or drag any pictures directly across to a folder visible in the left pane in the same way that you move files when organising your work.

After you have finished editing your pictures, or if you want to work on them from their new locations at a later stage, you could then clear the memory card by selecting all the unwanted images and the originals of those you have now saved elsewhere and deleting them by pressing your *Delete* key.

Toolbars and menus

Once the image opens fully, you will see that a program such as *Paint Shop Pro* has a huge range of tools available. Don't be too worried at this stage as you cannot hope to master more than the very basic tools without spending many hours 'playing' with the software. This chapter will introduce you to just a limited range of options that you should find easy and helpful to use.

Cropping

It is quite common to be unhappy with the composition of your picture when you see it on screen. A quick way to improve things is to cut out unwanted sections by cropping. Click the *Cropping* toolbar button and then draw round the area of the picture you want to keep. Double-click your mouse inside the area and the unwanted sections will disappear. If you are happy with the new image, click the *Save* button to update the picture.

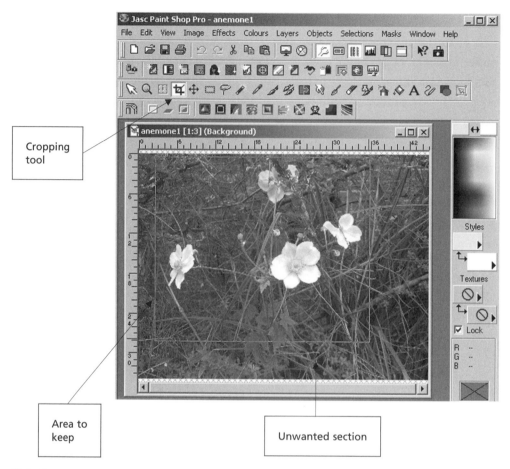

Cropping
tool

Area to
keep

Unwanted section

Rotating

You may have taken a picture with the camera held on its side, or decide it would
look better at a different angle. Rotate the image by opening the **Image** menu and
selecting *Flip* to turn it upside down, *Mirror* to create a mirror image or *Rotate* and
setting the angle and direction of rotation.

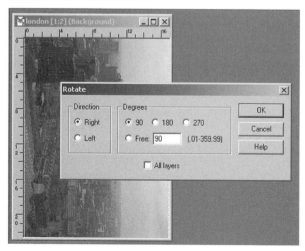

Adding text

To add a title or other text to your picture, you must click the *Text* tool button 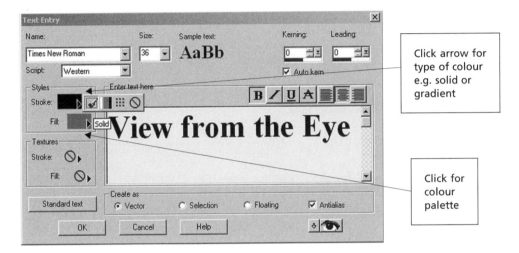 and then click on the image. This opens a text editing window and you can type your text into the main area.

Change the colour of the line (stroke) or fill of your letters from the Styles box – select a solid or gradient type of fill by clicking the arrow for the options, and a different colour by clicking in the box to open up the colour palette.

Click *OK* to see your text appear on the image. This can be dragged into position and resized by dragging a corner sizing handle.

Automatic adjustments

Some pictures would be improved if colour saturation, contrast or brightness were altered, or scratches or red-eye removed. All these changes can be carried out from the **Effects – Enhance Photo** options.

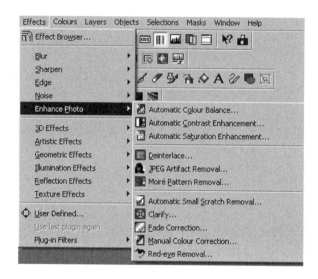

If you want to change only part of the image, first select it using one of the selecting tools. To take off the selection, right-click the image or go to **Selections – Select None**.

Select standard shaped area

Lasso to select irregular areas

Choose an option from the menu e.g. Automatic Contrast Enhancement and preview the changes in the right-hand window when the dialog box opens. Adjust the view in the window using the zoom or clicking the move button and dragging the image with the mouse. You can manually alter any settings if you are not happy with the defaults before clicking *OK*.

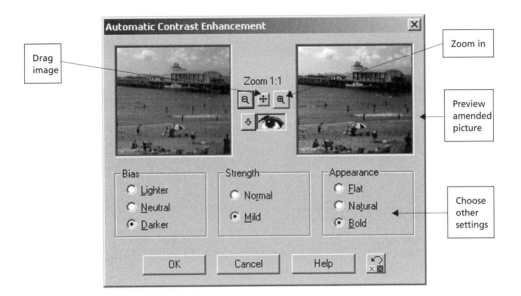

Effects

For a quick way to change the picture out of all recognition, click the *Effects Browser* button. You can now preview a range of different effects from minor blurring or sharpening to creating strange shapes, or applying painting styles, stained glass or tiled effects to your image.

Resizing

You may need to create an image of a set size: open the **Image – Resize** dialog box and make your changes here, making sure you keep the aspect ratio fixed so that the picture does not get out of proportion. You can change actual measurements or simply reduce the picture e.g. to 50% of the original.

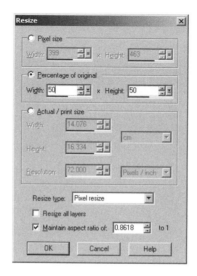

Printing

As well as normal printing onto the appropriate type or size of paper, you may want to organise a number of images to print out on a single page. Do this by opening all the pictures you want to include and then going to **File – Print Multiple Images**. Your pictures will appear as thumbnails down the left-hand side of the page. Drag them

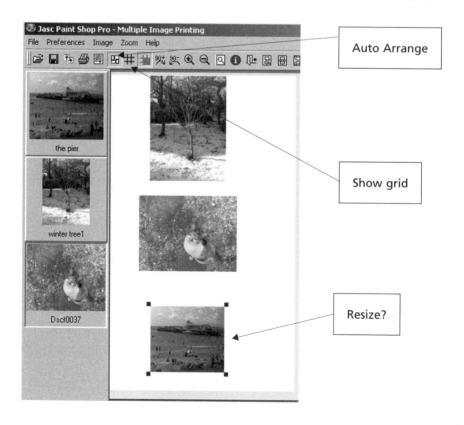

onto the page and organise them yourself or click the Auto Arrange button. You can also resize any picture to make sure it fits the page and display a grid to help you with positioning.

For *Windows XP* machines, you can also use the facility offered by the *Windows Picture* and *Fax Viewer* to organise a number of pictures on the page. Having opened a picture using this program (selected by right-clicking and choosing *Open with...*), click the *Print* button to start the Wizard.

Start print wizard

Select some or all the pictures displayed and then decide on an appropriate layout before printing.

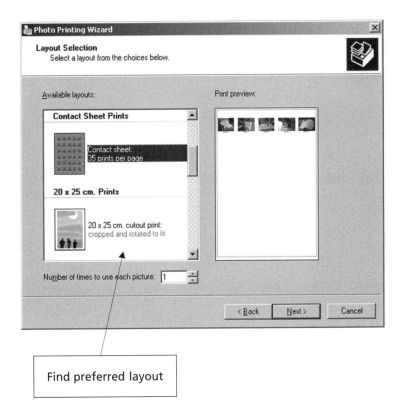

Find preferred layout

10

Scanners

There are a number of occasions when you may need to scan in blocks of text or images from the printed page. Using a scanner allows you to add them as objects to your own documents or even turn them into word processed text that can be edited using OCR technology (Optical Character Recognition).

Scanners come in different shapes and styles but the most common are flat bed scanners. They can be used to scan single sheets of paper or, with the lid left up, large books or other solid objects. They work by dragging an array of sensors across the underside of the paper that has been placed face-down on the glass plate. You can scan in black and white, greyscale or colour and modern machines can even scan items such as slides and negatives.

The quality of the image depends on the resolution, or number of dots (pixels) per inch. If the default settings do not give a clear enough image, you will need to experiment with different resolutions, but for most text to be readable is likely to need to be scanned at 300dpi. This chapter shows how to use *HP Director*, but your own scanner will offer similar menus and facilities.

OPTICAL CHARACTER RECOGNITION (OCR)

To use typed words, place the page face down on the glass plate of your scanner and close the lid. Double-click the scanner icon or find the program from the **Start** menu. Click the *Scan Document* option.

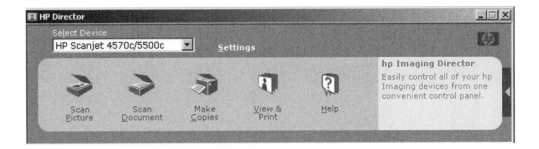

In the next window, click the *Editable Text* option (unless you want to save time and scan text and any images together) and choose the option to place the text in a new *Word* document ready for editing.

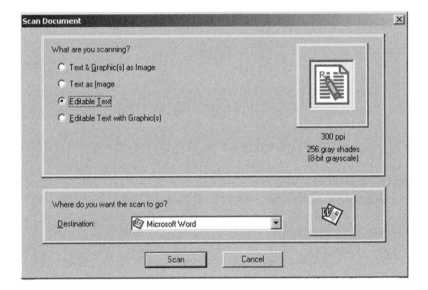

Click the button labelled *Scan* and you will hear the scanner start up and the light source and sensors will be dragged across the underside of the page. You will be offered a preview of the document and may want to make one or two adjustments e.g. reduce the size of the area to be scanned or alter the contrast or resolution.

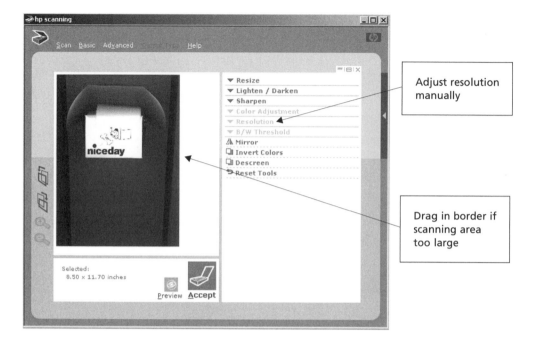

When you are happy with the preview, click *Accept* to scan fully. The text will appear on a new *Word* page and you can now work with it using normal toolbar and menu options.

Take care with the file, though, as it will have been given an arbitrary filename e.g. SCAN001001 – save it again to make sure you can retrieve it easily.

TO SCAN A PICTURE

Follow the steps above, but select *Scan Picture* or a graphics option.

A thumbnail of the image will appear in the Photo & Imaging Gallery and the default folder in which it will have been saved – a dated folder in My Pictures – will appear on the left of the screen.

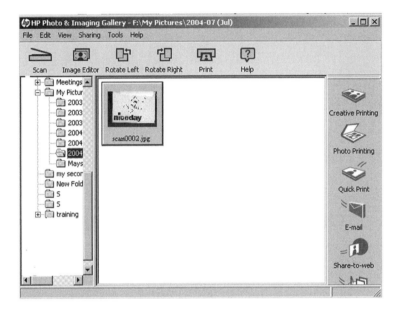

Image editing

Although there are some basic tools e.g. to enable you to rotate the image or print it directly, you will probably need to carry out further editing. Double-click the thumbnail or click *Image Editor* to open the picture fully.

You can add text by clicking *Add Title* and entering your words into the text box window. When they appear on the page, drag them into position. You can also remove unwanted sections of your picture: select the area to keep with the mouse or drag in the corners of the image before clicking the *Crop* button.

To change colours or rotate or sharpen the image, click the appropriate button and then use the menus and sliding scales that will appear to amend any settings.

Before making changes, it's a good idea to save the original image. Later, you could use the *Save As* option to save an amended version or simply update the original.

ADD IMAGES TO OTHER DOCUMENTS

To use all or part of the image elsewhere, select it with the mouse pointer showing a cross – the unwanted part will appear grey – and then click *Copy*. Open up the destination document, right-click on the page and select *Paste*.

Copy to memory

Creating Your Own CDs

$$\textcircled{11}$$

You have only to lose important files once to know that keeping copies as a backup somewhere safe, preferably not on the same machine, is sensible and necessary.

Up until a few years ago, you would have been told to keep copies of any important files not backed up automatically by your IT department on a floppy disk. Nowadays there are two main reasons why you need to learn how to create your own CDs instead:

1. In many organisations, the use of floppy disks is actively discouraged and the drives are being removed from computers or not included with new machines. To make copies of any important files, you will now have to copy them onto optical disks as the only real alternative.
2. A floppy disk can hold only 1.4 MB of data, whereas a CD can hold over 600 times as much. For large databases, images or files they are now the best way to keep and transfer copies safely.

At work, you are unlikely to need to create audio CDs, so this chapter concentrates on ways to create backup copies of your data files.

HOW CDS ARE CREATED

The technology used to create a CD involves burning the data onto a disk using a laser. As well as the (D:) drive where you insert CD-ROMs containing programs and files you want to view or install on your computer, your machine should have a further drive – commonly the (E:) drive which enables you to 'burn' or write your own disks.

Types of CD
There are two different types of CD that you can write: CD-R and CD-RW.

CD-R or Recordable CDs are cheaper, smaller and are used for permanent archiving of files as they can only be written to once. They can be read by most CD drives and are quite cheap to buy.

CD-RW or Writeable CDs are more useful if you want to continue working on your files, as they can be written to up to 100 times. Once files have been copied on to the disk, updates will overwrite older files with the same name, so that you can always keep the latest versions. The disks are far more expensive to buy and can often only be read if you have a Recordable CD drive on your machine.

USING *WINDOWS XP*

To burn a file onto a CD, first insert the disk into your recordable CD drive. This may open the CD directly or offer a window that has a range of options. Unless you want to check the current contents, you can close the window and simply locate the files you want to copy from My Computer.

Having found the file(s), click the *Copy this file* link.

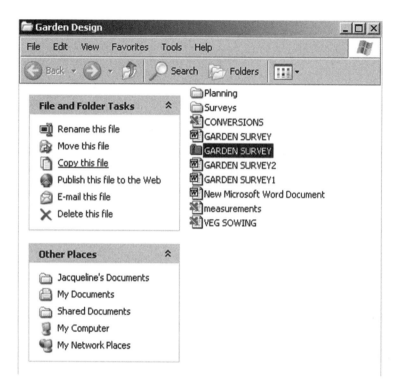

Select the recordable CD drive in the next window and click the *Copy* button.

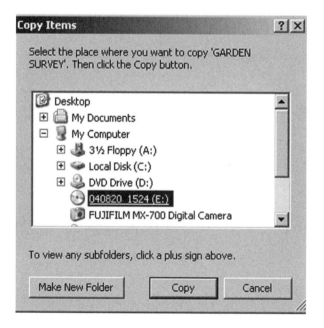

A message will appear at the bottom of the screen saying you have files to copy to your CD, so click this to view the files.

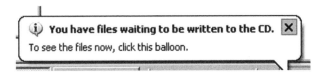

Your new files will appear faded, and you will also see any files currently on the CD displayed in the window.

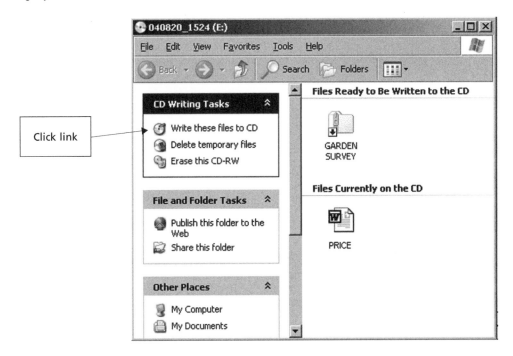

Click the *Write these files to CD* link and wait for the Wizard to take you through the process. In the first window, name the CD (if you prefer to see a name when searching the disk in future) and then click *Next*.

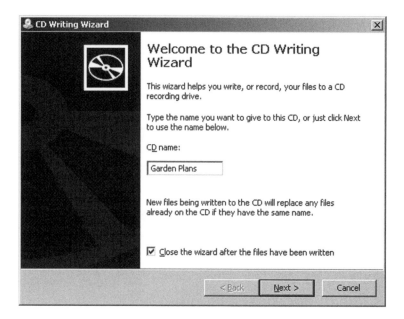

The files will now be written to the CD.

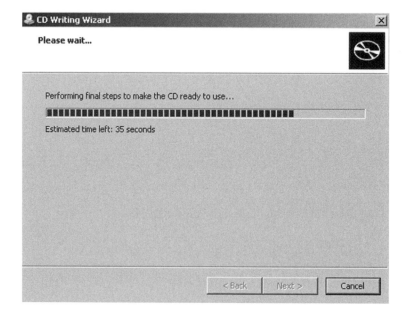

When the process is complete, the disk will be ejected from the drive.

ALTERNATIVE SOFTWARE

There are many CD/DVD recording software programs available: some are free or inexpensive and can be downloaded from the Internet, or your employer may buy a fuller version that offers many extra features. They all work in a similar way: after opening the program and choosing to create a data CD, you are offered two panes – one displaying the files on your computer and the other the layout of the files you wish to copy. Simply locate and drag your files into the layout area and then click the button to begin copying.

One program is *CD-Maker 2000 Plus* and to use this you would start by opening the program and selecting the type of CD you want to create e.g. Data CD.

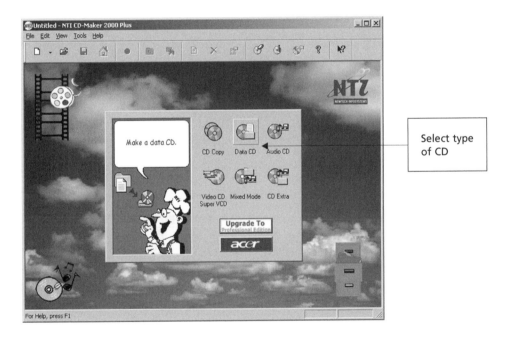

In the next window, locate your files using the *Windows Explorer* pane and drag them onto the Data Track Layout pane.

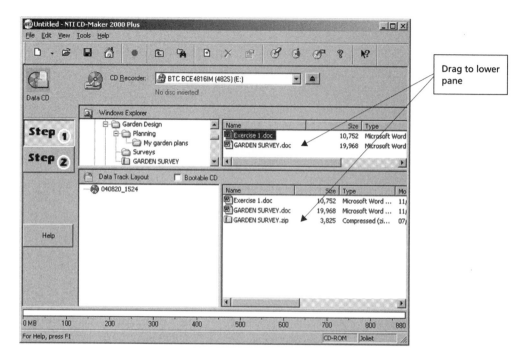

Insert your CD-R or CD-RW into the recordable CD drive e.g. (E:) so that it is displayed in the CD Recorder window, and check that it is recordable and there is space available.

Click the Step 2 button and accept or change the writing speed before clicking *Start*. For most purposes, it is sensible to accept any default settings.

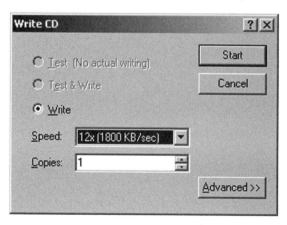

A window will now show the copying process, so do not attempt to eject the disk at this stage.

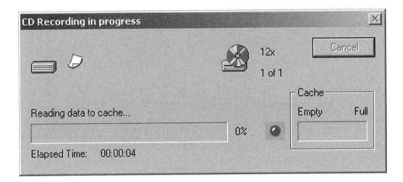

When completed, you will see a confirmation window showing that the data has been copied successfully and your disk will now be ejected.

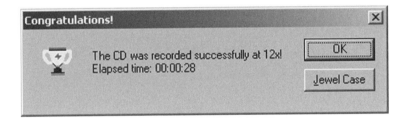

Presentations

$$\left(12\right)$$

A presentation package such as *PowerPoint* allows you to produce slides that can be printed out onto paper or acetate sheets, or run as a slide show on the computer. The slides can contain text, pictures, coloured backgrounds or charts and, on the computer, can include sound effects and moving images.

For anyone who doesn't like public speaking, using a computerised presentation package has many advantages:

◆ Creating colourful slides with sound effects and animations means the audience's attention is off the speaker;

◆ There is no danger of dropping notes or getting slides out of order;

◆ Built-in design templates allow the author to create professional-looking slides very easily;

◆ Speakers can build up slide contents gradually and use on-screen pens for writing, so the experience can be very like using more familiar overhead projectors or flipcharts;

◆ Presentations can be easily adapted for different audiences and run automatically e.g. in an exhibition or conference hall;

◆ Thumbnails of the slides can be printed as handouts for the audience, and notes pages can be prepared for the speaker as an aide memoir.

Although you may not give talks yourself, it is quite common to be asked to help a colleague create a presentation, print out handouts or notes or make changes to the original. You therefore need to know your way around the package so that you can carry out these tasks with confidence.

MANAGING SLIDES

When you open a *PowerPoint* file or start a new blank presentation, you see the file in Normal view. The window is divided into three panes and you can drag out any of the boundaries to work within a larger sector or close e.g. the Outline pane if it is not required so that you are only viewing the slide (previously known as Slide view). Choose between:

1. The main 'page' or slide where you add your text, pictures and backgrounds etc.
2. The text-only part of the presentation referred to as the Outline (in XP this alternates with thumbnail pictures of the slides); and
3. An area where you can type in speaker's notes and print them out below a small picture of the selected slide.

The number of the slide you are viewing shows at the bottom of the screen.

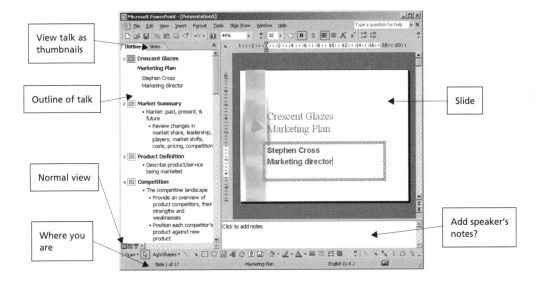

There are several ways to open a different slide on screen: use your Page Up or Down keys; click the numbered slide in *Outline* or the thumbnail on the Slide tab; or click the scroll bar arrow or double arrow navigation buttons on the right of the slide showing on screen.

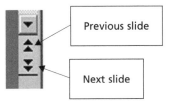

Slide order

The easiest way to re-order slides in a long presentation is to view them in Slide Sorter view – available from a button in the bottom, left-hand corner of the screen or from the **View** menu – or on the Slide tab. Drag any slide to a new position with the mouse. When a vertical line moving with your pointer is in the correct position, let go the mouse and the slide will drop in place.

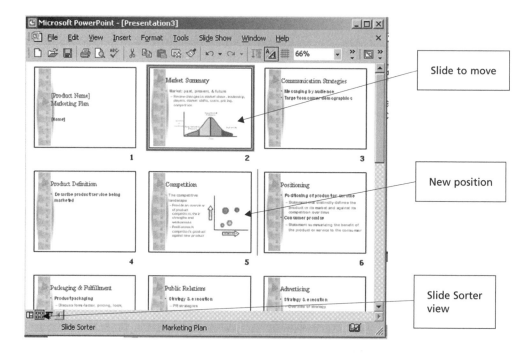

New slides

Add a new slide by clicking a thumbnail on the Slide tab and pressing *Enter*. You can also add a new slide if in Slide view by clicking the *New Slide* button on the toolbar. The new slide will be the next in number.

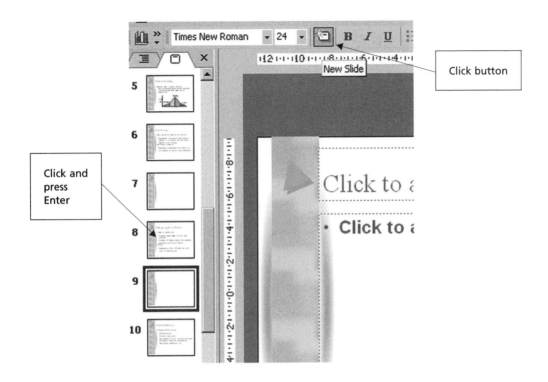

MAKING CHANGES

Text

Text entries on a slide are always positioned within a box. Some slide layouts are provided with boxes already in place where they are known as placeholders. To add text, simply click the box and start typing. To remove a box, click the outside edge and press *Delete*. To add text to an empty space, click the Text box button on the Drawing toolbar and draw your own box before entering text inside it.

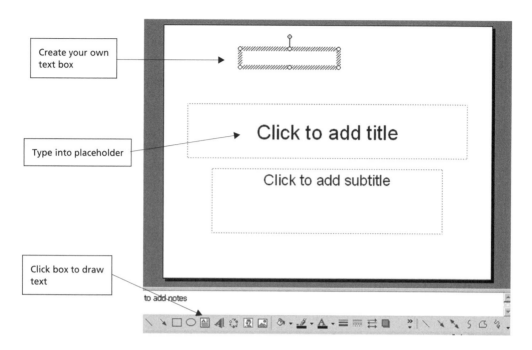

Once the text appears, format it using the normal toolbar buttons. You can align text within the box or drag the box to a new position on the screen.

Although the text box border will not show automatically, you may want to emphasise it. Change the thickness, colour and style of line, and fill the box with colours, patterns or gradients by choosing from options on the toolbar.

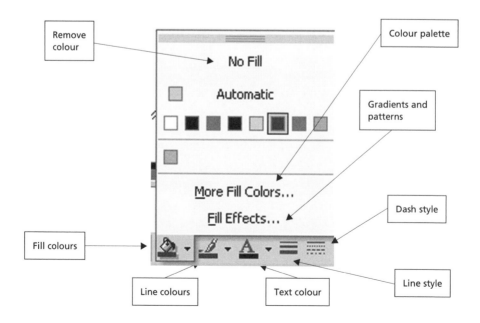

Text levels

In a similar way to using outline numbering (see Chapter 3), you can create different levels of text on a slide easily in *Outline* view.

1. Having started a presentation and selected your slide layout, click to place the cursor next to slide no. 1 and type the top level heading.
2. Press *Enter*. This creates slide no. 2.

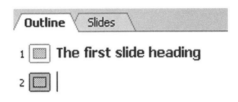

3. If you wanted to add text at a lower level on slide 1, press the *tab key*. This takes the text *down* a level and you can start typing the subtitle or first list item. Alternatively, click the *Demote* button .

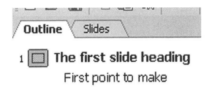

4. Keep pressing *tab* or the *Demote* button on the toolbar to move even lower.
5. Press *Enter* to continue typing a new line at the same level.
6. Press *tab* as you hold down Shift and you will move *up* the levels again. Alternatively press the *Promote* button on the toolbar. Eventually you will reach the top level and will create a new slide.

Objects

You can add *Clip Art*, saved pictures, sound or movie clips, diagrams, charts or tables using the buttons on the Drawing or Standard toolbars or via the **Insert** menu. You can also select a slide layout with a shortcut to these objects. Display the range of different layouts by selecting the option on the **Format** menu.

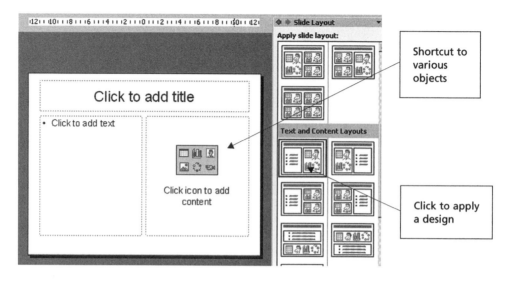

Once the object is in place, move it, delete it, use the resizing handles or double-click to be offered a range of formatting options.

Diagrams

These are new for *Office XP* and offer a variety of diagrams including an Organisation Chart that is also available in *Office 2000* and is used to create a family tree or hierarchy on the slide.

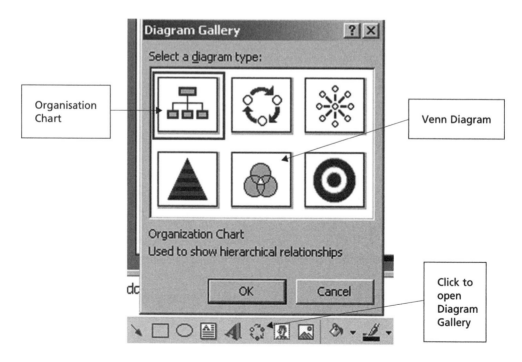

When the basic chart appears, click any box and then select a shape from the Insert Shape menu to add a new box in the appropriate position.

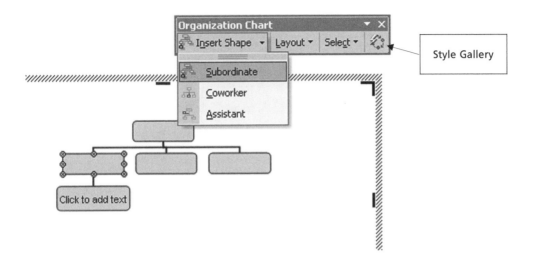

Click each box to add your text and format the lines and fill for the boxes using the toolbar buttons on the Drawing toolbar. As an alternative, you could also select a complete design from the Style Gallery.

Charts

Click this option to open a 3-D column chart and a sample spreadsheet. Replace the data and choose a different chart type or add titles etc. from the **Chart** menu. As you will be offered toolbar buttons and menus similar to those in *Excel*, you can work with the chart in the same way as described in Chapter 4.

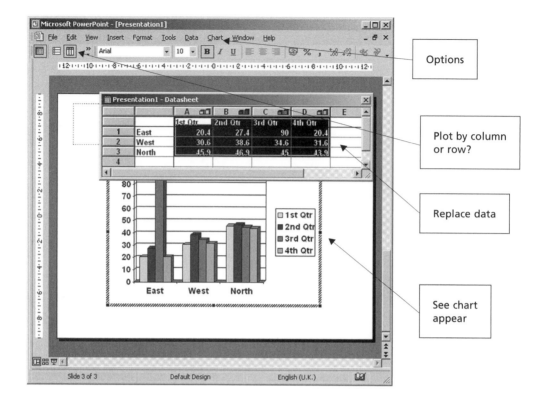

Click outside the chart area to return to the slide and double-click the chart to continue editing.

BACKGROUNDS

Rather than creating a presentation based on white slides, you can colour your backgrounds, add drawn objects or you may prefer to select a professional design from those available.

Colours and fills

To add colours, patterns, textures, pictures or gradients, right-click a slide or open the **Format** menu and select **Background**. In the dialog box, click the arrow in the small window and select the palette (*More Colors*) or *Fill Effects*.

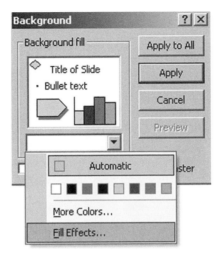

If you choose *More Colors*, click any colour on the palette to apply this to the background.

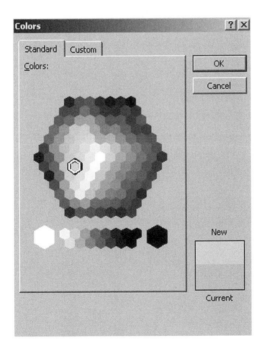

Fill Effects offers a number of tabs – create your own patterns or gradients by mixing colours in different ways or choose natural-looking marble, wood or material background effects from the texture selection.

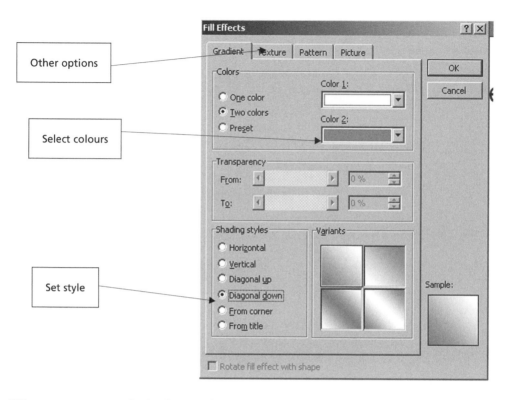

When you return to the background dialog box, you will see your chosen background together with colours automatically selected for titles and main text that are combined into a Color Scheme. This can be accepted or you can choose alternatives by selecting a different scheme from the **Format – Slide Design** task pane.

When changing slide backgrounds, apply them to individual slides or to the complete presentation.

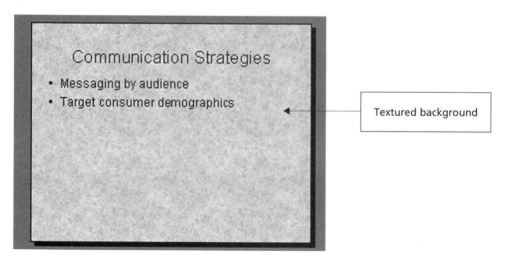

Design templates

To apply a complete design that includes borders or drawings, go to **Format – Slide Design** and click *Design Templates*. Scroll through those offered and click one to apply it to your slides. If you want to change a design that has already been applied, simply select a new one from the list.

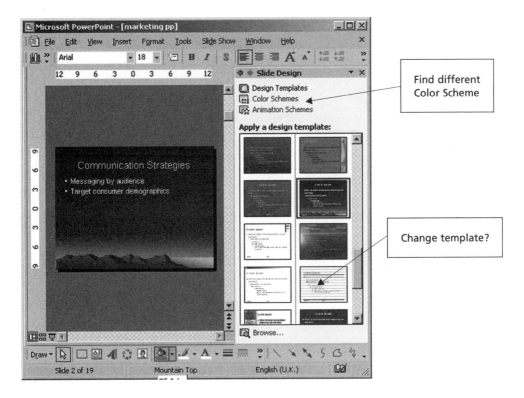

Drawings

You may have a particular border or shape in mind that you want to add to one or more slides but which is not offered in the templates. Instead, you can click one of the shape buttons on the Drawing toolbar and draw and colour your own objects.

1. Click an *AutoShape* button
2. Drag your mouse across the slide to add the shape
3. Resize or move it in the same way as any other object
4. Colour the lines or fill with patterns/colours using the toolbar buttons on the Drawing toolbar. You will also find 3-D and shading options to try.

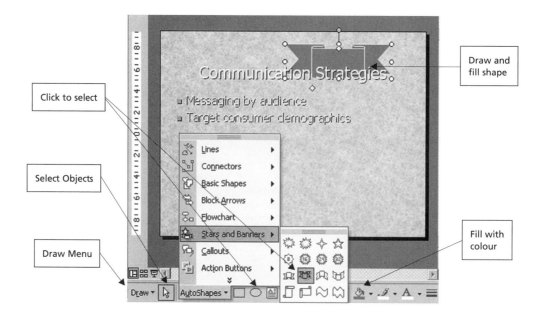

Two useful tricks with shapes: open the **Draw** menu and select **Order – Send to Back** if you want them behind text or other objects; and select several shapes with the Select Objects arrow (or click each when holding down the Ctrl key), then go to **Draw – Group** to group them into a single entity that can be copied, moved or resized as one object.

SPEAKER'S NOTES

Either use the lower pane in Normal view or select **Notes Page** from the **View** menu. You can now type accompanying notes. The words plus a small picture of the slide will be printed if you select this option in the Print dialog box.

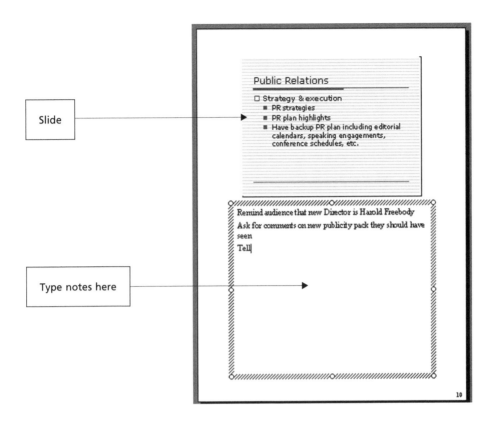

MASTER SLIDES

You may be asked to make changes to a slide but find you cannot access the text or object! This is because it has been added to the 'background' of the slide, which is like a template – anything on it cannot be changed in normal view.

To work on this part of the presentation, you need to go to the **Master – Slide Master** view, available from the **View** menu. Any changes to the Slide Master will affect all the slides, so it is the place to add logos, page numbers, dates etc. that you want on every slide without needing to make these additions to slides individually. You can also set new sizes and formatting for titles, sub-titles and bullets if you do not like the defaults but have not already changed them on the slides themselves.

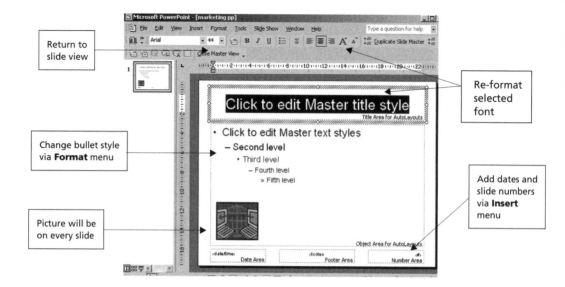

PowerPoint presentations offer one slide layout that differs from the rest. This is the Title slide and you may be asked to work on a presentation that has this type of slide as the first slide. If you change the Slide Master it may *not* be affected so you must either use the Title Slide Master or change the single slide manually.

PRINTING

There are several different ways you can print out a copy of your presentation: all or selected slides, a notes page for selected slides, thumbnails arranged e.g. 3 or 6 to a page to give to the audience as a handout, or the presentation outline. Open the **Print** dialog box from the **File** menu and select the slides to be printed together with the actual print option.

The dialog box labels read:
- Which slides?
- Object to print
- Check first
- Layout

SLIDE SHOWS

The *2002* version of *PowerPoint* has a staggering range of effects that can be applied to your slides if you plan to run the presentation on the computer.

To see how the presentation looks before adding any effects, click the *Slide Show* button. Menus and toolbars will disappear and you can step through the slides by clicking the mouse or using the Page Up or Down keys. To return to Normal view before reaching the end, press the *Esc* key at the top, left of the keyboard.

A common task is to take a laptop and projector with you to a different site and set up a show there. You therefore need to familiarise yourself with your particular projector i.e. how it is connected and controlled.

Timings
Although you can set the time slides are on screen individually, one option on the **Slide Show** menu is to rehearse the timings of the whole show at a single run-through. Click the **Rehearse Timings** option to start at the first slide and display a counter in the top, left hand corner of the screen.

After the first slide has been on screen for an acceptable interval, click the *Next* button and work your way through the show. At the end, the timings you have set for each slide can be saved.

If you want a continuous presentation running in the room, select **Set Up Show.** Click the *Loop* option and also make sure slides will appear automatically.

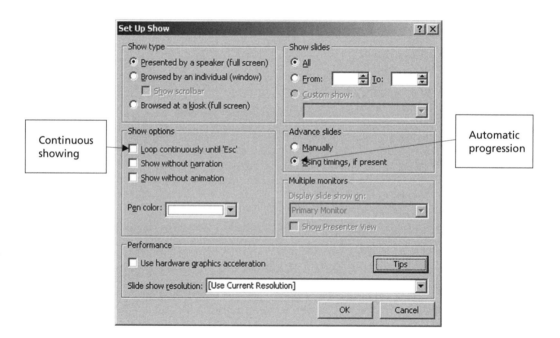

Effects

There are two major choices to make when running your show on a computer: how you want one or more slides to replace the previous one – transitions – and how objects will arrive on a slide – animations/build. In each case, you can add sound effects and also set a specific waiting time before the slide or object appears automatically.

Transitions

Choose a view such as Slide Sorter and right-click for the menu option **Slide Transitions**. In the Transitions pane, click an effect and it will preview on the selected slide. (To apply the same effect to several slides at once, select them by holding Ctrl as you click each one.) You have the option to speed up the transition, accompany it with sound effects, set a time for the next slide to appear and apply the same effect to all the slides or just the selected one. If you want to see how the transition appears in a slide show, click the button but remember that the show will start with the selected slide.

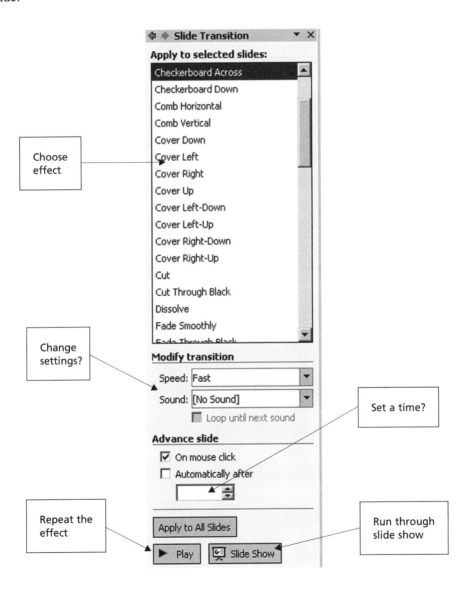

Animations (builds)

If your slide includes text, the words can appear letter by letter or list items can arrive one after the other; if it has drawings or pictures, these can fly, crawl, spiral or drop onto the slide; and you can decide the order in which all the objects will appear on any slide.

To apply animations, display a slide and then open the **Slide Show** menu. For a pre-set effect that applies to the whole slide, select **Animation Schemes** and select one of the options e.g. fade in, dissolve or compress.

For more control, select **Custom Animation**. Each object will be numbered and you can apply a different effect to each line, word or object. These can include different ways the objects will arrive or exit the slide and the actual path they will take.

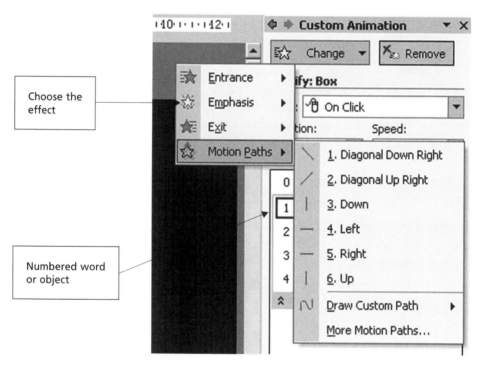

The animations you choose will be displayed in the animation pane, and if you want to change anything, drag them to a new position in the list or right-click or click the drop down arrow and select another option. You can also take off an effect by clicking *Remove* – very useful if an effect has been applied and the speaker now doesn't want it included!

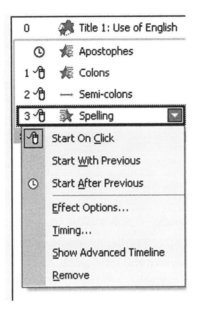

Changing slide display

Presentations are often created that will be shown to different audiences e.g. members of staff within the organisation as well as the general public. It is likely that some of the slides are not appropriate for all audiences, and there are two different methods for removing slides temporarily from a slide show:

Hiding

Any slide can be hidden so that it does not appear in a show or on printed handouts. In Slide Sorter view or on the Slide tab, click the slide you want to remove and then open the **Slide Show** menu and click the **Hide Slide** option. In Slide Sorter view, you will see a line through the number of the slide.

If printing handouts, make sure you take off the tick in the checkbox.

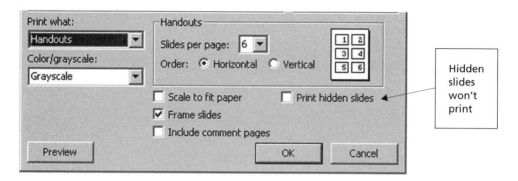

Hyperlinks

As an alternative to hiding slides, you can add a link to one slide which, when clicked, will jump to another place in the show, thus missing out slides you don't want displayed. You can either select text or objects to act as clickable links or add an action button.

1. To use text or an object on the screen, select it on the slide and then click the Insert Hyperlink button or go to **Insert – Hyperlink**.
2. When the dialog box opens, click *Place in this Document.* All the slides will be listed and you can click the slide you want to jump to when the word is clicked on screen.

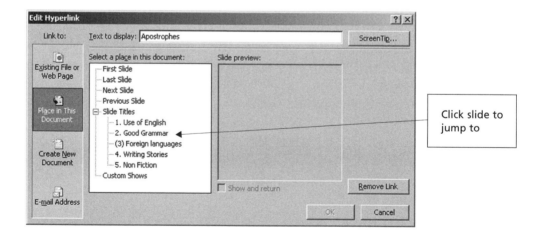

3. Test the link in a slide show – your mouse should show a hand when it hovers over the clickable text and the correct slide should be displayed.

4. If you want an actual button to click, draw one after selecting from the *AutoShapes – Action Buttons* display.

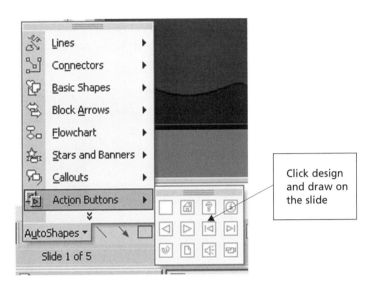

5. This automatically opens the dialog box where you can select which slide to move to when the button is clicked.

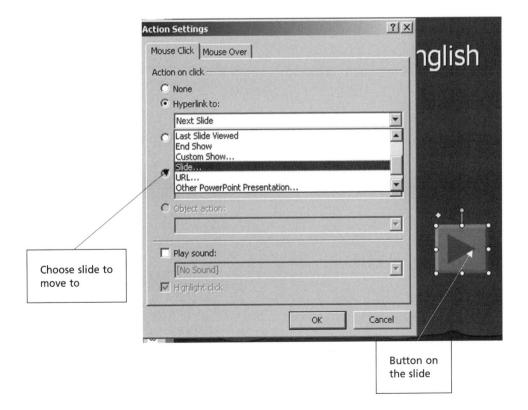

Finally, you can treat the slide show rather like a flip chart or blackboard: in Slide Show view, right-click the screen, select **Pointer Options** and choose the Pen or even choose a different pen colour. You can now 'draw' on the slide to emphasise a particular point. Press *Esc* when you want to stop the pen working. The same menu can also be used to navigate to different slides or end the show altogether.

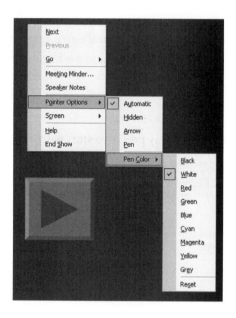

Desktop Publishing

For jobs that involve creating publicity materials on a regular basis, you are likely to be provided with a dedicated desktop publishing package such as *Publisher*.

When you open *Publisher*, you are offered a range of publications including news-letters, brochures, greetings cards, flyers (small advertisements) or business cards that you can customise, although you may prefer to start with a new, blank page.

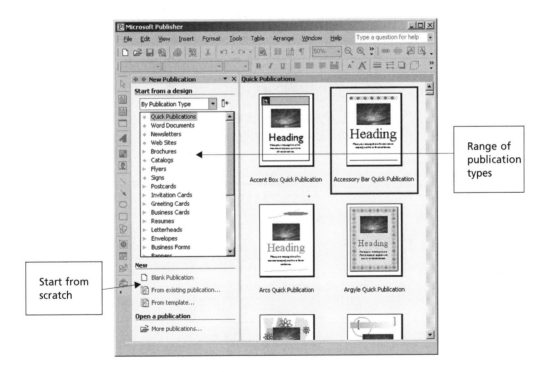

Start from scratch

Range of publication types

THE BASICS

Publisher is very like *PowerPoint* or *Word* – it offers a variety of drawing tools that you can use to add text, pictures or drawn shapes to the page. Click the tool and draw a box (often referred to as a frame) on the page. In some cases e.g. *Word Art* or *Clip*

Art, the gallery will open automatically but otherwise, type in your text or double-click inside the box to browse for pictures. All added items can be resized, dragged to new positions and formatted to enhance the appearance of your publication. For example, two useful toolbar buttons allow you to increase or decrease the size of the font in steps, so that you can see when the text is just the correct size.

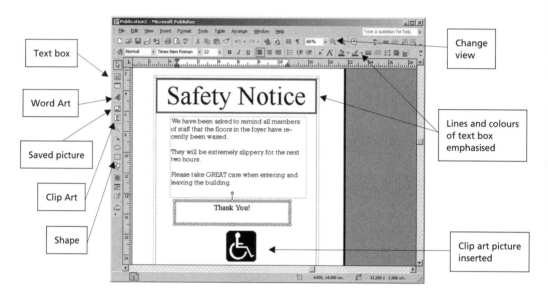

One change from word processing is that your view is often at a very low magnification, so that you can see how the whole page is looking. Change the magnification figure, click a *Zoom* button or press function key F9 to move in for detailed work.

Pages

At the bottom of the screen, you will see a number in a shaded box. This is the page currently on screen. For brochures, newsletters or leaflets, add extra pages from the **Insert** menu and click the number to work on that page.

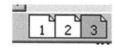

Columns

Within any text box, you can display the contents in columns. Right-click the box and select **Format Text Box** before clicking the *Text Box* tab and then click the *Columns* button. Set the number of columns and increase the space between columns if necessary for a clearer display.

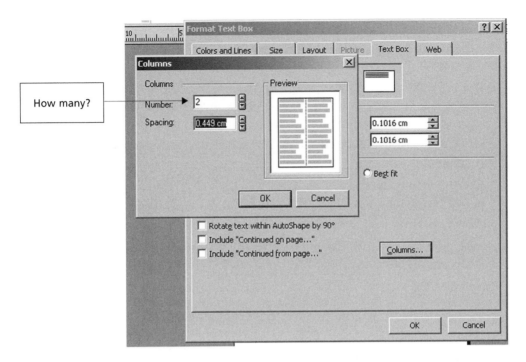

When you return to the publication, you may need to increase the size of the font to fill the space more evenly. If you overdo this, you will see an overflow symbol showing that not all the contents can now be displayed. Either increase the size of the text box or decrease the font again so that all the text fits inside.

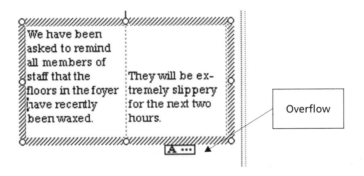

Linking text boxes

Instead of typing all the contents of your publications, it is very likely that items will be provided by colleagues as text files. These can be inserted directly into a text box if you open the **Insert** menu and select **Text File.**

For publications that spread over several pages, it is common to continue a long item on a later page, and you can control the process by linking text boxes and 'pouring' in the extra text.

1. Draw your first text box and insert the file. You will see the overflow symbol showing that some of the text does not fit.
2. Move to the second page and draw a new text box where you want the item to continue.
3. Return to the original box, click it and then click the *Create Text Box* Link button on the toolbar.
4. When you hover over the second text box, your pointer will now display a pitcher. When you click the mouse, the extra text will be poured into the box and a navigation button will appear. Clicking this takes you back to the earlier text.

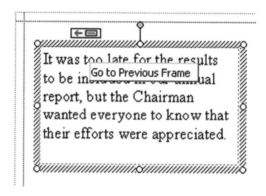

5. For printed publications, you can add extra text at the top or bottom of linked boxes saying '*continued on (or from) page . . .*' by selecting these options from the **Format Text Box** dialog box.

USING READY-MADE DESIGNS

If you want to create complex publications and base them on designs in the application, you need to select the publication type in the list of designs and then click on your preferred style showing in the main window.

A limited range of options will now be presented to you.

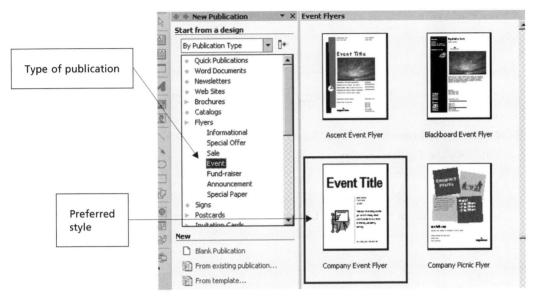

◆ *Publisher* allows you to store information about yourself or your organisation that can be extracted and added to any publications you create. To set up the information, click *OK* when offered the option and complete the various boxes.

If you have more than one role in the organisation, create several different businesses and then click *Update* to store the data.

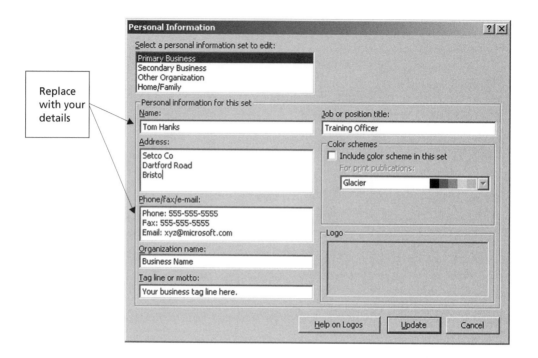

◆ When you return to the publication, you can change a limited number of basic design features e.g. colour schemes, font types or layout. Click the relevant underlined text and choose from the list offered in the options pane before previewing the effects.

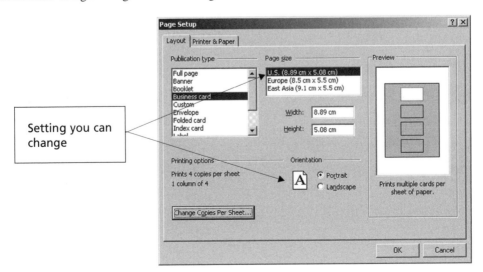

Adding or amending the contents

From this point, you must replace the contents of your publication manually with the text and graphics you want to include. Click any text currently in place and type over as normal, and add extra text boxes in empty parts of the page. Double-click a picture to open the Search pane and find an alternative from the *Clip Art* gallery and delete, move or re-colour any drawn shapes such as lines or rectangles.

Printing

Some publications can be folded in different ways, or may need to be printed on specially sized paper or card. You can adjust any of the settings in the **File – Page Setup** window although you may also be offered some options when creating a publication using a design in the catalogue.

PDF files

Many documents are converted to a special file type – Portable Document Format or PDF, which allows them to be published on the Web or sent via e-mail in an exact format that cannot be altered but which can be read by any computer and which will always print out as intended. They are also compressible and will be smaller than the same file created as a *Word* document.

You will find PDF file formats used particularly for manuals, timetables, charts and complex forms and the files, which can be downloaded, saved on your computer and read using the appropriate software, appear on Web pages displaying a red icon. They usually show the size of the file, to give you an idea of how long it would take to download:

 3328k

The Adobe Reader needed to view such files is free to download from the Web. You will see the link to the Website on many pages that provide PDF files for downloading if your machine does not already have the software installed:

Once you have the Reader on your computer, you will find that PDF files open automatically when double-clicked and don't require you to first open the program.

DOWNLOADING PDF FILES

When you want to read a PDF file that you plan to save on your computer, it is a good idea not to waste time opening it directly into your browser from the Web. Instead, right-click the file and select the option to *Save Target As* ... This will open a save dialog box and you can specify where the file will be saved.

Clicking *OK* will start the process and, depending on the size of the file, may take a while.

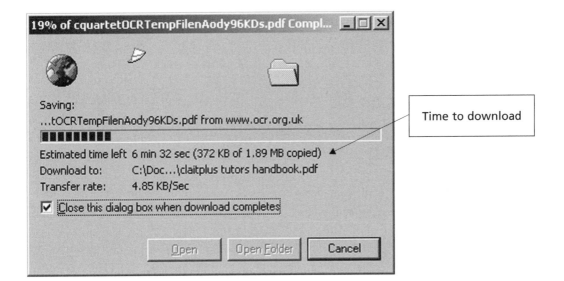

Once you have saved your PDF files, they will appear in My Documents or your chosen sub-folder displaying the distinct red icon. Double-click any icon to open the file.

MOVING THROUGH A DOCUMENT

When the file opens, you may see different displays: thumbnails showing each page as a rectangle, bookmarks showing pages in a hierarchy, or simply the main first page. Move to other pages by clicking the arrow at the bottom of the screen or on the toolbar, or click the thumbnail or page on the left.

If you do not want the left-hand pane displayed, click the *Show/Hide Navigation Pane* button.

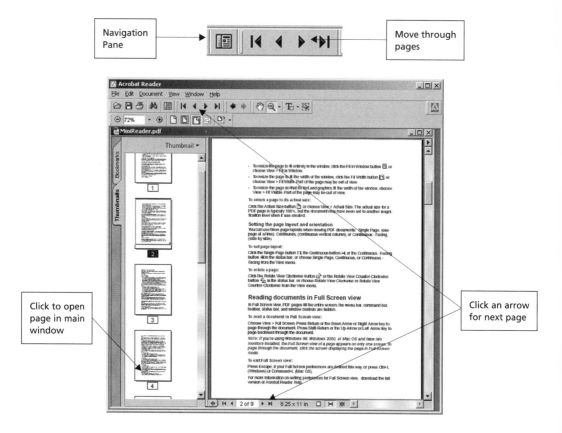

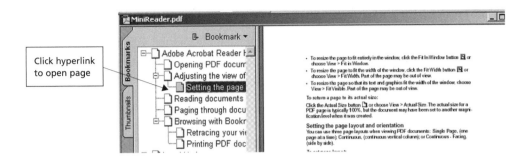

Click hyperlink to open page

To go to a particular page, select the page number showing at the bottom of the screen e.g. *2 of 29*, type over this the number of the page you wish to jump to and press *Enter*.

VIEWS

Sometimes, the text is too small to read comfortably. View the contents at different magnifications by clicking the *Zoom In* or *Zoom Out* Tool and then clicking the page with the mouse.

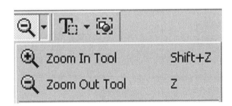

There are other buttons and options on the **View** menu including full screen (press *Escape* to return to the normal view and toolbars), different page widths, single or continuous pages, and the option to rotate the page. If you enlarge the page too much to see it all, click the button showing a hand and you will be able to drag the page around the screen.

Magnification

Page width

COPYING CONTENTS OF A PDF FILE

You have all the normal facilities in later versions of Adobe Reader to print all or selected pages or save copies of the file, but using part of the contents in other documents (if there are no copyright restrictions) can be tricky.

To copy text that can be word processed, click the *Text Select Tool* and then drag the mouse over the block of text before right-clicking or clicking **Edit – Copy**. When the words are pasted into your new document, you should be able to treat them as normal word processed text.

To copy a picture or any textual part of the document as an image, first click the *Graphics Select* Tool . Now when the selected block is copied and pasted, it will show the black border and sizing handles round the edge just like any other image.

	SEPTEMBER			
Sunday	4	11	18	25
Monday	5	12	19	26
Tuesday	6	13	20	27
Wednesday	7	14	21	28
Thursday	1	8	15	22	29
Friday	2	9	16	23	30
Saturday	3	10	17	24	1

Relevant qualifications

Having looked through this book, you may feel that you would like to attend an IT class where you would have the support of a tutor and could gain a qualification recognised by employers.

At the present time, there are three types of computing course that are ideal for women returning to work or anyone hoping to develop their career. All are accepted by employers as an indication of computer literacy, and they are usually available on a part-time basis or are built into longer courses that also include networking, careers guidance and job search techniques.

Organisations running these courses include Colleges of Further Education, University Continuing Education Departments and Adult Education/Lifelong Learning Departments within local authorities. The courses last from a few weeks to a whole year, depending on the number of modules you decide to take and the level of the course; they are available as daytime or evening classes and are usually free or fairly inexpensive. There is also the option to take some of the courses online in your own home where you will have tutor support via the telephone or e-mail.

NEW CLAIT

The examining body OCR offers a 3-tier qualification: Level 1 (New CLAIT), Level 2 (CLAIT Plus) and Level 3 (Advanced CLAIT). All the syllabus details can be found at www.ocr.org.uk.

CLAIT stands for Computer Literacy and Information Technology, and the Level 1 qualification, New CLAIT, requires a pass in 4 units chosen from word processing, spreadsheets, charts, presentations, desktop publishing, e-mail and the Internet (or Becoming Webwise – provided by the BBC and taken online), computer art, presentations and databases. There is also a mandatory unit on using a computer.

Gaining the certificate involves working though 2-hour assignments that test your basic understanding of the chosen software e.g. the word processing unit asks you to type out a short article accurately, format the text, replace words, move a block of text to a new position and print hard copies of your work.

ECDL

The European Computer Driving Licence is a longer course as you must pass all 7 units to gain the full certificate and each unit is broader in scope than the equivalent in New CLAIT. It is therefore seen as nearer to the OCR Level 2 course, CLAIT Plus. The units are: word processing, spreadsheets, file management, databases, presentations, e-mail and the Internet and basic concepts of IT. Full details of the latest ECDL syllabus can be found at www.ecdl.com.

In theory, you can simply register to take the test when you feel you have mastered any unit, but most people attend training centres where they work through self-study modules or are taught normally before sitting the test. Each test is often taken and marked on-line so that you receive the results immediately after you finish. You will have a 'logbook' and this is stamped each time you complete a unit so that you can build up to the final qualification over time.

OPEN COLLEGE NETWORK

A third organisation that accredits computing courses is the National Open College Network found at www.nocn.org.uk. Many colleges or community education centres offer courses that are locally assessed by OCN and you may like the idea of gaining the qualification by building up a portfolio of work during your studies.

It is difficult to say which courses will be available as they can cover anything from very basic word processing to advanced desktop publishing or web page design: provision will depend on demand in your area and the expertise of the teaching staff.

LEARNDIRECT

To find out about computing courses in your area or those that may be available over the Internet, a good place to start is LearnDirect which can be contacted on Tel: 0800 100 900 or found at www.learndirect.co.uk.

This organisation offers a searchable database of many hundreds of UK courses available through taught classes or via the Internet, and has centres where you can study in person.

LearnDirect also provides courses of its own but these do not lead to recognised qualifications. However, they are tied in with those already mentioned such as the ECDL, New CLAIT and CLAIT Plus so that, having finished a LearnDirect course you may feel ready to attempt one of these widely recognised qualifications.

Index

absolute cell reference, 97
add logo, 34
add primary key, 142
add records, 126
add text to a slide, 227
animations, 242
apostrophe, 30
appointments, 164
archive messages, 182
arrange windows, 107
attach a file to an e-mail, 175
automatic corrections, 38
AutoShapes, 235
average, 91

backgrounds, 232
backup, 216
BODMAS, 86
borders, 76
browser, 150

calculations in tables, 68
Calendar, 164
CD-R, 216
CD-RW, 216
change capitals, 40
change default settings, 18
charts, 115
CLAIT, 259
colon, 30
columns in spreadsheets, 95
columns, 76
compressing files, 192
computer literacy, 1

confidential messages, 174
Contacts, 164
controls, 140
convert text into tables, 70
copy cells, 94
copy database records, 144
count, 92
create a CD, 216
create a folder, 7
create a new message, 172
cropping, 203

data series, 104
dates, 40
delete columns or rows, 96
delete messages, 181
design templates, 235
desktop publishing, 247
detect settings, 83
diagrams, 230
digital cameras, 200
domain name, 153
downloading, 150
dropped capital, 72

ECDL, 260
edit scanned image, 213
e-mail address, 172
envelopes and labels, 47
events, 164

Favourites, 156
field properties, 126
file messages, 181

fix cell addresses, 97
format bullets and numbering, 77
Format Painter, 60
formatting cells, 99
forms, 130
Formula bar, 85
forward a message, 175
freeze headings, 104
Function keys, 14
functions, 90

gridlines, 102
group mailing list, 170

header or footer in Excel, 123
headers and footers, 51
Help, 25
hide slide, 243
History, 159

IF function, 92
image file formats, 201
import a text file, 55
import data, 145
import data into spreadsheet, 94
import images, 55
import objects, 56
index, 60
insert Clip Art, 72
insert columns or rows, 95
insert hyperlink, 244
Internet, 149
Intranet, 150

junk mail, 190

LearnDirect, 261
levels of text on a slide, 229
link tables, 142
linking text boxes, 249
logging in, 5

macros, 80
Mail merge, 41
master slide, 237
maximum, 92
meetings, 164
message rules, 185
minimum, 92
minutes, 47
missing toolbar, 16
missing toolbar button, 16
move files, 9
move text, 52

name a cell, 97
name sheets, 106
new slide, 226
normal view, 225
Notes, 169
Number pad, 13

OCN, 260
on-screen pen, 246
open a different slide, 225
open an attachment, 178
open with, 34
Optical Character Recognition, 210
organisation chart, 230
organise the display, 22
Out of Office message, 180
Outlook, 161
overtyping, 14

page break, 54
page numbers, 50
page view, 23
password, 5
PDF files, 254
percentages, 87
Pivot table, 111
placeholders, 227
primary key, 125
print presentation, 238

print publications, 253
protecting cells, 89

queries, 130

recurrent appointments, 165
removable storage media, 196
remove image hyperlink, 75
re-order slides, 226
replace words, 53
reply, 174
reports, 136
request a receipt, 180
resolution, 200
rotate an image, 204

Save As, 12
save web page, 151
save web picture, 152
scanners, 210
search, 19
Search Engine, 154
search spreadsheets, 107
semi-colon, 29
signatures, 178
Slide Master, 237
Slide Show, 239
Slide Sorter view, 226
sort records, 129
sort spreadsheet data, 108
sort table entries, 68
speaker's notes, 236

spelling, 50
spreadsheet forms, 109
spreadsheets, 85
styles, 57

table of contents, 58
tables, 64
tabs, 62
tasks, 168
templates, 31
text box columns, 248
tick, 103
totals, 91
track changes, 61
transitions, 241

URL, 152
use data from different sheets or files, 106
username, 5

video conferencing, 159
voting button, 180

watermark, 36
web page address, 152
WinZip, 196
WordArt, 78
World Wide Web, 149

zipping files, 192

If you want to know how . . . to become a touch typist

'Almost everyone today has to use a keyboard. Of course it is possible to use two fingers, or even three and stumble along making lots of mistakes and taking an age to type a single document. But there is a better way. Why not learn to touch type? Just think, a few hours now will teach you a skill that will be with you for life. What have you got to lose? Take the book home and start working through it today. By this time next week your hard work will be paying off.'

Ann Dobson

Touch Typing in Ten Hours
Spend a few hours now and gain a valuable skill for life
Ann Dobson

'It works! Even if you are a two-fingered, search-and-hunt, typist you can learn to touch type if you follow the ten one-hour exercises.' – *Writers' News*

'This is a very useful book indeed.' – *Reach*

'Liberate your fingers with this easy to follow book. The lessons are split into one hour chunks and, if you master one a week (easy), you'll be competent in less than three months.' – *Writers' Bulletin*

ISBN 1 85703 827 4

If you want to know how . . . to enjoy your return to work

'After you've been out of work for some time, it's easy to forget that you've got skills and qualities to offer. For many the thought of returning to work becomes increasingly fraught with potential problems. Maybe you've been out of the workplace for some time for reasons other than raising a family and every time you see yourself at work, you also see a barrier. So here's some good news. There are more opportunities to start careers afresh, as more people change career or return to work. There's more help out there for those seeking to run their own businesses or who've been out of work for some time, and there's help for those wanting to retrain and change from one way of life to another.

'Look on your return to work as a challenge to rise to and an adventure to enjoy.'

Sally Longson

Returning to Work
A guide to re-entering the job market
Sally Longson

'An absolute must for anyone who feels they wish to discover their potential and begin a new phase of life.' – *Institute of Management*

'Good sound advice that is valuable not only to women returners but also to anyone seeking work or new directions as a whole. . . . a useful read and a helpful guide.' – *T Magazine*

ISBN 1 85703 924 6

If you want to know how . . . to change your career for the better

'We owe it to ourselves and to our families to find rewarding careers as part of a balanced life. A successful career move involves people matching their ideas, passions and goals to the needs of employers and vice versa. People need jobs and jobs need people. This book is to help people take a new look at themselves and supply them with the tools they need to make their career move – to a place where they can satisfy most of their needs and some of their wants. Whatever move you want to make it has to start from a basis of self-knowledge. An understanding of your needs and wants, and knowledge of what you can contribute.

'There is a secret to successful job search. It is persistence. Seek and you shall find.'

Graham Green

The Career Change Handbook
Find out what you're good at and enjoy; and get someone to pay you for it. It's as simple and as difficult as that
Graham Green

'Interesting and to the point advice.' – *The Guardian*

'There is little of the silly and trivial advice often found in career advice books. *The Career Change Handbook* gives incisive advice.' – *Tyrone Times*

ISBN 1 85703 958 0

If you want to know how . . . to successfully apply for a job

'Being successful in a fiercely competitive jobs market takes time and effort. Spurring a recruiter into wanting to know more about you is the secret of success with any application. Each one must be special: it has to say – 'Here I am. This is what I can offer you.' This book is designed to help you present your skills in a practical and marketable manner and ultimately achieve your goal. How you approach this crucial first stage is vitally important, only successful applications lead to interviews.'

Judith Johnstone

The Job Application Handbook
A systematic guide to applying for a job
Judith Johnstone

Whether you're leaving university, re-entering the job market, facing redundancy or simply wanting a change, this handbook reveals the best ways to approach potential employers.

'A great buy. It reiterates points which need to be repeated and gives practical advice on job finding.' – *Office Secretary Magazine*

'Laden with common sense...particularly useful for first-timers.' – *MC, University College Dublin*

ISBN 1 85703 992 0

If you want to know how . . . to prepare for interviews

'It's the interviewer's prerogative to throw just about any question they can think of at the interviewee. So you might think that it's almost impossible to prepare for an interview. But the truth is that 80% of interview questions revolve around 20 common themes. And many interviewees let themselves down by not thinking about these themes, preparing and rehearsing responses to them.

'Many candidates then go on to create a wrong impression. Remember that an interviewer has to *like* you and warm to you as a person, as well as want to work with you because you answer the questions well. I see too many candidates who talk too much or come across as nervous or unfriendly. If you get the chance to rehearse with a friend and get some feedback on just how you come across, you will improve your chances no end.'

Rob Yeung

Successful Interviews – Every Time
Rob Yeung

'*Successful Interviews* is the type of book that one may not wish to share with others who are job seeking in competition with oneself. Nevertheless, I owe a debt of gratitude to Dr Rob Yeung for sharing his experiences with us . . .'
– S. Lewis, Coventry

'This book is an invaluable source of information for job hunters on preparing for interviews, tests and assessment centres.' *– Jonathan Turpin, Chief Executive of job hunting website fish4jobs.co.uk*

ISBN 1 85703 978 5

If you want to know how . . . to use your time more effectively

'Time Creation will, literally, change your life if you put it into practice. It will change it for the better. Improve your use of time and you will cease to be one of life's headless chickens who dash around looking busy and achieving little, and become one of its laidback bears who really get things done and enjoy life at the same time.'

Gordon Wainwright

Headless Chickens, Laidback Bears
Use scientific techniques to create more time and revolutionise your life and work
Gordon Wainwright

'Offers a scientifically based set of techniques that can help people achieve up to a 100 percent increase in speed without any loss of quality in performance, saving precious minutes and hours and freeing up valuable time for other activities.' – *Professional Manager*

This book presents the twelve basic Time Creation techniques and shows you how to use them. It identifies the problems you may encounter and suggests ways of overcoming them. It also shows you how Time Creation can be applied to a variety of essential skills, taking care to focus on improving speed while maintaining quality.

ISBN 1 85703 973 4

If you want to know how . . . to read faster and recall more

In today's information laden world, time is valuable. Reports, reference books, contracts, correspondence, newspapers, magazines and journals are just some of the things you might need to read and digest on a daily basis.

If you feel that the speed at which you read these items and the extent to which you are able to retain their information could be improved, then the use of the practical tips, proven techniques and numerous practise exercises in this book could help you to reach your potential. With the aid of this invaluable book, you can save time and achieve more.

Read Faster, Recall More
Use proven techniques for speed reading and maximum recall
Gordon Wainwright

'. . . will help you to reduce the time spent on reading and recalling information.' – *Evening Standard*

'. . . purely practical and aims to help you in the professional environment.' – *The Times*

'A worthwhile investment.' – *The Guardian*

ISBN 1 85703 936 X

If you want to know how . . . to write with confidence

'This book will offer practical help and guidance to all who lack confidence when faced with everyday writing tasks, whether it is having to reply to a formal wedding invitation, compiling a CV, or completing a job application form. Everyday situations are discussed and sample responses provided. This book shows you what to do, so you can go away and do it yourself.'

Angela Burt

Write with Confidence
Solutions and examples for everyday writing needs
Angela Burt

'Everyday writing has its own rules. It needs to be framed in a conventional way, so you need to know the conventions; it needs to be set out in a formal manner, so you need to know the construction. Angela Burt shows just how it should be done.' – *Writers' News*

'A very useful book, no matter what your problem.' – *Expos'd*

'A very useful guide to getting in right!' – *Changes*

ISBN 1 85703 894 0

If you want to know how . . . to improve your punctuation and grammar

'Do you have trouble with punctuation? Are you frustrated when you can't remember whether to use a comma or a full stop? Do you have difficulty in constructing a sentence that sounds right? If so, then this book should help you. Written in an easy-to-read style, it takes you through the basics of English grammar After reading this book you will never again use a comma instead of a full stop!.'

Marion Field

Improve Your Punctuation and Grammar
Master the essentials of the English language and write with greater confidence
Marion Field

'An invaluable guide...after reading this book, you will never again find yourself using a comma instead of a semi-colon.' – *London Evening Standard*

'I realised for the first time that grammar is actually fascinating...you are given the facts in plain English – no waffle, no padding, just the details you really need...a fascinating and readable book.' – *Writing Magazine*

'This book does exactly what it says on the front cover: it helps you master the basics of the English language and write with greater confidence and clarity.' – *MS London*

ISBN 1 85703 873 8

How To Books are available through all good bookshops, or you can order direct from us through Grantham Book Services.

Tel: +44 (0)1476 541080
Fax: +44 (0)1476 541061
Email: orders@gbs.tbs-ltd.co.uk

Or via our website

www.howtobooks.co.uk

To order via any of these methods please quote the title(s) of the book(s) and your credit card number together with its expiry date.

For further information about our books and catalogue, please contact:

How To Books
3 Newtec Place
Magdalen Road
Oxford OX4 1RE

Visit our web site at

www.howtobooks.co.uk

Or you can contact us by email at info@howtobooks.co.uk